Better Homes and G

Roses

You Can Grow

Printed in the United States of America. First Edition. First Printing.
Library of Congress Catalog Card Number: 78-56620
ISBN: 0-696-00255-8

BETTER HOMES AND GARDENS BOOKS

Editor: Gerald Knox
Art Director:
  Ernest Shelton
Associate Art Director:
  Randall Yontz
Production and
Copy Editors:
  Paul Kitzke
  David Kirchner
Garden and Outdoor
Living Editor:
  Beverly Garrett
Garden Book Editor:
  Marjorie Groves
Associate Garden Editor:
  Douglas Jimerson

Roses You Can Grow
Editor: Ann Reilly
Senior Graphic Designer:
  Harijs Priekulis
Rose Book Designer:
  Faith Berven
Graphic Designers:
  Sheryl Veenschoten
  Rich Lewis
  Neoma Alt West
  Linda Ford

CONTENTS

The Wonder of Roses

Unchallenged elegance, pure radiance, thorned vitality, and delicate petals simulating silk and satin make the rose the unequaled "Queen of the Garden Flowers." No other flower gives such an array of shape, size, fragrance, and color.

More than any of the world's flowers, the rose has captured the esteem of man and captivated the hearts and souls of all. No other flower has so magnificently passed the tests of time. No other flower so beautifully says, "I love you."

The Charisma
of the Rose

Eglantine, named for the flower of poets, was the 19th-century literary hostess who rewarded her writers with a gold rose.

The Eglantine or sweetbrier rose, Rosa eglanteria, with its apple-scented foliage, is the wild rose of lyric and legend still growing in gardens old and new.

Throughout history, no flower has been so loved by man, so revered, so renowned, or so admired as the rose. It is older than the human hands that first drew pictures of it; fossils of roses from our Northwest date back 35 million years. The rose apparently originated in Central Asia about 60 million years ago, spreading over the entire northern hemisphere (no wild roses have ever been found to grow below the equator). Five thousand years ago, the Chinese appreciated its value and cultivated it widely, as have many other past civilizations.

Ancient history is filled with references to the rose. It is said to have grown in the Garden of Eden, ancient Persia, and the Hanging Gardens of Babylon. Frescoes with roses have been found, some dating back to 1,600 B.C. Cleopatra welcomed Marc Antony in a room filled with rose petals, and legend says that Nero once spent the equivalent of $150,000 for roses to use at a party. Emperor Heliogabalus is reputed to have had so many rose petals in one room that his guests suffocated in them.

In ancient Greece and other countries, the rose had a powerful mystique. The symbol of the city Rhodes was this revered flower, which still grows in abundance on that island today.

The Romans loved roses in a more physical way, using them in candy, wine, pudding, garlands, and rose water. For them it became a symbol of debauchery and secrecy—the origin of the term "sub rosa." Rose growing was a profitable living in pre-Christian Italy, and the Romans also imported many cut roses from Egypt.

In Greece and Rome, the rose was the flower of Aphrodite (Venus in Rome), the goddess of love and beauty. Even today, the rose characterizes womanly perfection and the mysteries of love.

Early historians, scientists, and men of the arts wrote of its beauty and charm. During the Middle Ages, the rose became valued for extracts used in various medicines and ointments. Its petals have been used for potpourri and its hips as a source of vitamin C.

Early on, the rose was an intricate part of the Christian religion. Christians used roses to symbolize the Trinity, chose the white rose for the Virgin Mary, and gave its name to the rosary. A legend claims the brier rose sprang from Christ's blood as he wore the crown of thorns. The Vatican used the rose as a model for a papal award given to men who had done a service for the Church. The rose's petalled shape contributed to the magnificent stained glass windows in many cathedrals.

Soldiers throughout history have followed banners decorated with the rose. In his epic work, the *Iliad,* Homer tells us that the rose adorned the shield of Achilles and the helmet of Hector. A well-known historical event, England's War of the Roses, started in 1455 when the house of Lancaster feuded with the house of York. The red rose of Lancaster *(R. gallica)* and the white rose of York *(R. alba)* soon became the symbols of this war that ended in 1486 when Princess Elizabeth of York married Henry Tudor, a Lancastrian. In 1551, the red and white, two-tone rose, York and Lancaster *(R. damascena versicolor),* was so named to memorialize the war.

No flower is more steeped in folklore and legend than the rose. In the United States, the American Indians tell several tales about the Cherokee rose and its origins. The Grant rose, which has a heavy and unpleasant odor, is said to have sprung from the blood of a Mrs. Grant, a Florida pioneer who was killed by Seminole Indians during an uprising. Columbus reportedly picked up a rose bush floating on the water the day before he discovered America in 1492, and the Virginians say their rose will die if transplanted to foreign shores.

The perfect flower of the rose has influenced fashion, interior design, and architecture. Sculptors, artists, and craftsmen have used it more than any flower; the most popular bloom adorning silver, china, and wallpaper is the rose. The rose has contributed its pure beauty to coats of arms, awards, currency, coins (some dating to Asia in 4,000 B.C.), emblems, medals, and stamps of some 42 countries. Four states, the District of Columbia, and England have chosen the rose as their official flower.

Roses have been immortalized in the arts for centuries. The earliest known painting of a rose dates to a 16th-century-B.C. rendition of *R. gallica.* Medieval tapestries are adorned with roses, and for Renaissance and impressionist artists, the rose was a favorite subject.

Poets and playwrights have used the rose in their romantic language of love. Sappho, the Greek poetess, first named the rose the "Queen of Flowers" in 600 B.C. Shakespeare, Omar Khayyam, Gertrude Stein, Robert Burns, and countless others have glorified the rose. Composers and balladeers have given the world thousands of songs romanticizing this most precious of flowers. Children reading "Alice in Wonderland" or "Beauty and the Beast" learn early of the role of roses in tradition and folklore.

Kings, queens, and presidents have long been associated with the rose. Legendary King Midas is said to have grown roses, as did Alexander the Great. In 1272, Edward I used the rose as a badge. Henry IV chose the red rose as his symbol; Queen Elizabeth placed the white rose on her banner. George Washington grew roses at his home; and after Franklin Roosevelt died, members of Congress wore white roses in mourning.

Modern history will long remember the story of Peace, hybridized by Meilland in France during the early days of World War II. He managed to ship budwood to the United States on the last plane before the fall of France in 1940. Bouquets of Peace were presented to delegates of 50 nations at the first U.N. conference in San Francisco—the day a truce was signed in Europe. The following August, on the day Peace was announced as an All-America Rose Selections (AARS) award winner, a cease-fire with Japan was signed.

Cut roses have always been used to mark special moments. A bouquet of red roses on Valentine's Day says, "I love you," and many a bride walks down the aisle with a bouquet of pure white roses.

Men have revered the rose so much they have named their children, their homes, and their colleges for it. This flower is the ultimate in beauty and perfection—this is the charisma and wonder of roses.

7

The History of the Rose

The basic ancestor of all modern roses is *Rosa gallica,* the French rose, the oldest known rose and one that once bloomed over the entire Mediterranean area. Its origins are unknown. From *R. gallica* came *R. damascena,* the damask rose, whose well-known fragrance has been a part of rose history since it first appeared about 500 B.C. Autumn damask, *R. damascena semperflorens,* thrilled Romans about the time of Christ because it was the first to bloom twice a year. *R. alba,* a cross of *R. damascena* and *R. canina,* dates to before the second century.

After the fall of the Roman Empire and before the Renaissance, the history of the rose is incomplete and clouded. The Christians of the Middle Ages, unlike their earlier counterparts who shunned the rose because it reminded them of pagan Rome, kept the rose alive in their gardens and in the symbolism of their religious beliefs.

Once considered an ancient rose, the cabbage rose, *Rosa centifolia,* is now thought to be a product of 17th-century Dutch rose growers. Its exact background is not known but is probably a complex hybrid of many ancient roses, including the gallicas, damasks, and albas. Its most famous sport is *R. centifolia muscosa,* the moss rose, which appeared about 1700 and is still grown and used in hybridizing.

A revolution in rose growing took place in Europe in the late 18th and early 19th centuries with the importation from the Orient of *R. chinensis,* the China rose and its close relative, *R. odorata,* the tea rose. Laying the foundation for today's roses, they exhibited continuous repeat bloom, a phenomenon then unknown in Europe. The foliage of the Chinas is almost evergreen; that of the tea rose is mildew-resistant. The most unfortunate characteristic the tea rose bestows upon its descendants is a lack of hardiness.

The China rose has also been called the Bengal rose because in 1789 it was found growing in Calcutta by a sea captain who afterward took a plant home to England.

The Empress Josephine did more to popularize and foster rose growing and hybridizing than anyone of her time. An ardent lover of the rose, she started a rose renaissance by attempting to grow every rose known to man in her garden at Malmaison. In the ten years between 1804 and 1814, she collected 250 different roses—gallicas, centifolias, moss roses, damasks, and Chinas. The reputation of this garden spread across Europe, igniting an interest that would eventually lead to the birth of the modern roses.

Pierre-Joseph Redouté, the Raphael of the rose, created exquisitely detailed watercolors of the roses in Josephine's garden. His work "Les Roses" is an unsurpassed reference work still used today.

The portlands were a new class of rose that came into existence about 1800, probably derived from a cross of the autumn damask with the China rose and *R. gallica.* Named for the Duchess of Portland, it was one of the first good garden hybrids and one of the first to show repeat bloom. Also known as the damask perpetuals, the portlands remained popular until the hybrid perpetual was introduced almost 40 years later.

Rosa x borboniana, the bourbon rose, was brought to Europe in 1817 from the island of Réunion (Bourbon) in the Indian Ocean. Its background is uncertain, but it is probably a natural hybrid of *R. chinensis* and *R. damascena semperflorens* (autumn damask). The bourbon rose quickly became the most popular rose of the time because of its recurrent bloom and because it was one of the first to combine the best of both the European and Oriental roses. The original bourbon, now lost, was a bright pink; one of its hybrids is a primary source of red in today's roses.

Other plants that arose from the Chinas and European roses were called the hybrid Chinas. Unlike their contemporaries, the bourbons, the hybrid Chinas were very tall and did not exhibit repeat bloom.

The American contribution to rose history is *R. noisettiana,* called the noisette rose, a cross between *R. moschata* and *R. chinensis* made by Champneys in Charleston, S.C., in 1812. Seedlings of it were sent to France by Noisette, whose family raised it and gave the new rose its name. Typical noisettes are usually tender, vigorous climbers or very bushy plants.

The line of modern roses began in 1838 with the introduction of the hybrid perpetual rose. A hybrid it truly was, for it had in it the blood of almost every rose known at that time—bourbons, damasks, Chinas, portlands, teas, and noisettes. The plants were extremely hardy; the flowers, large and very fragrant. Unfortunately, the bloom was not perpetual, but it was more frequent than other roses of the day. Hybrid perpetuals reached their height of popularity during the Victorian era in England, and, sad to say, most have disappeared from the scene, having given way to the hybrid teas and their more dependable repeat blooming cycle.

The beginning of a new era occurred in 1867 with the introduction of La France, the first hybrid tea. This crossing of a tea rose with a hybrid perpetual happened by chance in the garden of J. B. Guillot in France. The new roses were of a neater growing habit than the hybrid perpetuals, plus they were definitely more everblooming.

By the end of the 19th century, all the elements of the modern rose were present but one—there was no attractive yellow rose. In 1900, after 13 years of trying, Pernet Ducher introduced Soleil d'Or, a cross between a hybrid perpetual and persian yellow, a form of *R. foetida.* A range of colors never known before in modern roses came into being—gold, copper, orange, apricot. For 30 years, these roses formed a separate class known as the pernetianas, now merged with the hybrid teas.

Unfortunately, bad characteristics accompanied the good; with the new colors came foliage susceptible to disease and plants unable to withstand pruning. However, some of these faults gradually have been bred out.

The new hybrids resisted cold weather but had weak and spindly roots and no vigor. Grafting onto wild rose roots—especially *R. multiflora,* the Japanese rose, which had been

brought to Europe from the Orient prior to 1868—helped to solve the problem.

Climbers are a category rather than a class of rose. The first of the rambler type was Crimson Rambler (1893). Many ramblers grown today were produced from *R. wichuraiana* (1891); others descend from *R. multiflora*. Large-flowered types are sports of bush roses or have wide and varied parentage, with many recent kinds coming from *R. kordesi* (1952). The hybrid musks, introduced in the 1920s, are hardy shrubs and moderate climbers that are crosses between noisettes and *R. multiflora* ramblers.

In 1862, a famous French nurseryman and rose grower, Jean Sisley, received seeds of *R. multiflora*, which he grew and crossed with the Dwarf Pink China *(R. chinensis)*, producing a new class of roses known today as the polyantha. The first of these low-growing plants, smothered in clusters of small (one-inch) flowers, were Paquerette (1875) and Mignonette (1880).

In the beginning of the 20th century, a Danish rose breeder, Poulsen, crossed the polyantha and the hybrid tea and produced what is now known as the floribunda. Else Poulsen was the first of these new roses (1924) and, as the name implies, was covered with an abundance of flowers. From its hybrid tea parent, the rose inherited its height and long-cutting stems, characteristics that created a stir in rose circles.

In 1954, the grandiflora class was created for the rose, Queen Elizabeth, a cross between the hybrid tea and the floribunda. Grandifloras are taller and hardier than hybrid teas, with clusters of flowers exhibiting the classic hybrid tea forms, fragrance, and long-cutting stems.

The popular miniature rose of this century derives from *R. chinensis minima (R. rouletti)*, the fairy rose that reached Europe in 1815 from the island of Mauritius in the Indian Ocean. For some unknown reason, it disappeared and was thought lost until a rose of its type was found growing in a window box in Switzerland in the 1920s. Recent breeding has produced many new varieties of this tiny favorite by crossing it with both polyanthas and floribundas, also descended from the China strain. These new varieties, though small, are just as hardy and colorful as their taller cousins.

9

Roses' Role in the Garden

If your garden is bathed in at least six hours of sun a day, you should find a place in it for roses. Used alone or intermingled with other plants, the rose is unsurpassed in beauty and abundance of flowers.

No room for a formal rose garden? Don't worry. Roses don't need a special place for themselves but can be dotted here and there in many parts of the landscape. Shrub roses form the perfect backdrop for lower-growing plants in the border. Try them and floribundas, instead of other, more commonly used flowering material. You'll be pleased with the long season of colorful results.

Try roses in the perennial bed to bring a continuity of color from one blooming season to another. Low-growing floribundas or miniature roses are sensational finishing touches as edgings to perennial or shrub borders. Or mingle roses with bright annuals for a full season of color.

A bare slope can become a bank of flowers with roses as a ground cover. There's no more colorful way to bring life and beauty to dull spaces, to prevent erosion, or to smother weeds. If a sun-loving ground cover is what you need, try Max Graf, *Rosa wichuraiana*, Sea Foam, the miniature Red Cascade, or one of the ramblers. Many of these will root along their canes as they sprawl, making them seem more like vines than roses.

Imagine long slender buds gradually unfolding into exquisite, high-centered flowers whose perfectly arranged petals glisten in the morning dew. Imagine watching this miracle of nature while starting the day over a cup of coffee. Imagine resting at twilight watching the roses reflect the brilliance of the sunset. Roses not only enhance the beauty of the garden, they also enhance the view from within your home, so select their location carefully, with both places in mind at planting time.

No cut flower is more loved than the rose. Why not use your rose garden as a source of long-stemmed beauties for home or office bouquets and arrangements? The flowers' fragrance will fill and enrich the air of garden or home.

You don't need a lot of room to create beauty. Roses can be effective even in small places—surrounding the base of a flag pole, accenting a mailbox, decorating an outdoor light. Rock gardens are ideal spots for small polyanthas, floribundas, and especially minis, welcoming the season-long color so often lacking in this type of garden.

A traditional rose arbor, *opposite,* remains the perfect choice for a sun-filled garden. Both breezy and romantic, the lath shelter offers some shade itself; when embellished with a variety of climbers, it can be an old-fashioned focal point in the garden. Cautious gardeners cover the lathing with hardware cloth to protect the blooms from wind, rain, or hail damage.

The use of climbers extends far beyond the rose arbor. Train them along a split rail or picket fence to brighten up the wood and curve the straight lines. Espalier them against the side of a stockade fence or the wall of the house. Climbers can cover eaves and outline windows and doors, adding graceful color to the outside of the home and softening hard corners. Let climbing roses ramble up posts, cover old tree stumps, or spill over from the tops of stone walls.

Some climbers grow tall and erect: perfect for trellises, arches, and pergolas. Handel, Coral Dawn, and many of the Kordesi shrubs are among these pillar roses that also may be used in rose beds to break the monotonous pattern plants the same height can produce, if they are planted alone.

Roses are being used more and more in landscape design to define curves and soften harsh, modern lines. An informal grouping of roses can brighten up a corner of the garden that would otherwise receive little attention.

Tree roses bring needed height and accent to the garden. They may be used as formal specimens or underplanted with floribundas or annuals for a more informal look. If you plant them against a wall of a contrasting color, the beauty and form of the tree rose will stand out.

Plant roses in unlikely places, like along the driveway or behind the garage. Then collect their petals to make candy, wine, sachets, and potpourri.

If room permits, a formal rose garden is most striking. The shape is up to you and your imagination and may be round, square, rectangular, triangular. Keep it simple and it will be very dramatic. Edge it with boxwood, teucrium, annuals, or miniature roses, and use a statue, pottery, a pool, a fountain, or a tree rose as a focal point. Border the formal garden with evergreens, place it against a simple background, trim it with spring bulbs, and your picture is framed.

Miniature roses are playing a new and important role in the garden scene. Plant them in drifts to enhance the vista from the living areas; use them in mass instead of bedding plants. Children in your family? Give them a few plants and watch them thrill to cutting flowers from plants their size for friends, teacher, or grandmother. It's also one of the best ways to get them interested in gardening at an early age.

Using Roses

Barriers can be beautiful when they're alive and clothed with the constant color of roses. If a tall privacy screen is what you need to keep out intruders or block the view of motorists, neighbors, and nearby buildings, plant a hedge of shrub roses. All this and beauty, too—no other hedge can even begin to compete.

Plant a low-growing hedge of floribundas, polyanthas, or miniature roses to separate the patio from the lawn, creating a strip of color that will contrast with the sea of green. Their dense habit of growth makes them an ideal choice for framing the path to the front door, paralleling the driveway, or making a mark between your property and the sidewalk strollers. A hedge of roses between you and your next door neighbor is more attractive than a fence and has the advantage of being equally beautiful from both sides.

Unless your property is extremely large, avoid planting living hedges of *Rosa multiflora*, which become much too large and hard to control.

Nor is a hedge the place for a variety of colors. Stick to the planting of the same variety or at least varieties of the same color and size.

Roses for hedging purposes should be planted closer together than normal to ensure dense, floriferous growth. When they are lining paths or sidewalks, be sure to set them back far enough to protect passersby from thorny branches. Two to three feet back from the walkway is an acceptable distance. To insure uniform color and height, don't mix varieties in a hedge.

Outline your lawn with the beauty of F. J. Grootendorst. Dense and thorny, it helps to detour wandering pets.

A hedge of white floribundas, like Saratoga, extends a gracious invitation to wander down the garden path and beyond.

Using Roses

Roses at the entryway to a home are a cheery way to say, "Welcome" and "Come in." Whether it be one large plant or several smaller bushes, roses teamed with evergreens at the front door outline an inviting portico.

For an informal, asymmetrical look to your entryway, place a tree rose on only one side of the front door. Complement it with smaller-growing roses on the opposite side.

If you have a front porch or a back deck, let roses tie your garden to the house. Climbers can sprawl across the roof or overhang, spilling over into the outdoor living area, while lower levels can be filled with color from bush roses.

If slopes or large areas around your home are carpeted with evergreen ground covers, mix roses in with them to break up the single color and add a change in texture.

If you have a garden gate, spark it up with a planting of roses. Your family and friends will pass by and admire it every day.

The spot where the driveway swings into the street is ideal for a welcoming group of roses. Plant it with white or other light-colored roses, and it will stand out at night. A small brick wall and a spotlight will finish off the entrance planting.

Line a walk with a row or two of roses—a perfect path to stroll along. The bordering may be in a straight line or, for a more informal look, in scallops or gentle curves. Use one variety or choose two whose colors complement each other. In a two-deep border, the plants may be of the same height. Or place a low-grower (like Accent) along the walk, backed up by one that grows taller (like Sunsprite).

Tree roses are also effective lining a walk. Standing straight and tall, they give the path direction. To tone down their stiffness, combine them with mounds of lower-growing roses, annuals or perennials, or both. Or scatter them here and there for a change of pace.

Steps to the house or from one level of the garden to another are more than just useful when roses

Climbing Golden Showers creates an alluring archway of yellow.

highlight them with color. If the ground is level around steps leading to the front or back door, deck, or gazebo, plant taller roses at the rear and shorter ones at the front to follow the line. If the ground slopes with the steps, choose roses of the same height to create a wave of color. Sea Foam is a sight to behold, spilling its flowers over the ground and the steps.

Brighten a dark retaining wall by planting climbers atop it and letting them hang over. Train them down and help keep them in place by pegging the canes to the wall. For summer-long color, be sure to choose one of the everblooming varieties.

If you're building a brick or stone wall around your property or patio or next to your driveway, allow room to plant roses. Red Cascade, a climbing miniature, will be spectacular and graceful and will not obstruct the view.

Garden by the sea? Roses tolerate drying winds and salt spray. Those

that do best are the species and shrub roses: they are vigorous, easy to care for, and thrive in sandy soil.

Trailing roses such as Max Graf, *Rosa wichuriana,* or the hybrids of *Rosa rugosa* are perfect scrambling over ledges, holding sand dunes in place, or flanking steps to the beach.

Combine them with other seaside plants like bayberry, juniper, and pine to create irregular drifts of richly textured and contrasting foliage. Because these roses grow dense and thorny, they provide protection from trespassers along property lines.

Every home has the same problem—hiding eyesores like gas tanks and trash receptacles. A rosy solution is to place a trellis in front of the area and let climbers do the screening job. Planted in this manner, climbers will make taking out the trash a more pleasant burden. One or two shrub roses will also substitute nicely and be just as attractive.

And if you have a bare, unsightly, hard-to-plant slope, use miniatures as a hardy ground cover.

Bordering this walk with color are Sonoma, left, a salmon-pink floribunda, and Medallion, a hybrid tea of rich apricot.

Using Roses

Planting beds overflowing with the richness of roses can highlight any segment of the home or garden. When designing planting beds, place them where they will catch and hold the eye. Their uses are endless, from emphasizing the good features of a garden or house to camouflaging nearby eyesores.

Rose beds need only to be in sun and within reach of the garden hose. If possible, keep them away from competing large trees and shrubs. Soil near the foundation of the house is often dry because eaves and overhangs prevent rainwater from hitting it, so keep this in mind and plan to supplement natural moisture.

The shape of rose beds is up to your taste, ingenuity, and the land available to you. Formal beds blend best with period architecture; informal beds are in keeping with the more modern design of today's homes. Allow the beds to follow the lines of the house or curve them to break rigidity. So long as space isn't limited, place two or three rows of roses in your beds, particularly freestanding ones. Any less, and the resulting effect will be skimpy; any more, and it will be difficult to work or view the roses in the middle of the planting. There may be space for only one row of roses against the wall of a house or fence, but the background will still make it a startling sight.

To keep the colors from appearing spotty, plant varieties in pairs or trios.

When you use more than one variety, keep your eye on color harmony and place plants accordingly. Also, keep in mind the color of the wall or the fence the bed may be against, and choose roses whose hues will best stand out against it.

Height is another factor that must be considered when designing rose beds. If beds are planted against a backdrop, be sure to place the taller varieties in the back and work down to the shorter varieties in front. In freestanding rose beds, place the taller varieties toward the center so there will be an even view from all sides.

Planting beds around the house will dress it up and show everyone how much you care for the beautiful things in life. High traffic areas (the corners of a garage or the path to a patio) merit special attention and should be spotted with roses, if only a few. Your friends will do a double take when they walk by the luxurious blooms.

Just a couple of rose bushes can make the back or side door inviting. And with the plants so close to the house, it's easy to reach out and snip a few blooms for the guest room to make your visitors feel equally welcome inside.

Use a bed of roses to enliven a narrow strip of land between driveway and fence. Espalier climbers along the fence, or plant one or two tall tree roses. Lower-growing roses can be placed in front and the bed edged with minis or annuals. The fence will be turned into a wall of beautiful color.

Garden sheds storing tools, bicycles, furniture, and the like are often stark and unattractive. They needn't be. Transform them into rose-covered "cottages" by planting informal beds of roses around their perimeters. Soon after, you'll be rewarded with a tapestry of flowers that will brighten even the ugliest of buildings. This is also a good way to perk up a dull neighborhood.

First Prize and Smoky fill a corner.

Blooms of red Pharaoh contrast with salmon-pink of Laura.

Blue violas, assorted roses, and pots of gay petunias and geraniums give vertical color, interest, and life to a fence.

Using Roses

Roses naturally imply fragrance. Lovely to look at and lovely to smell, roses are perfect in beds near patios and terraces. But not all roses are fragrant, and some are much more so than others, so check descriptions carefully before buying roses of any kind.

If drainage is a problem in your area (and even if it isn't), raised beds are most attractive and come with built-in finished edging. For an informal, casual, and natural look, design them in flowing curves. Add a bench or two along the bed where you can sit and reap pleasure from your plantings.

When laying out planting beds, be sure to make provisions for paths in between them, whether of grass, brick, gravel, flagstone, or other paving material. Make paths wide enough so garden equipment such as lawnmowers and wheelbarrows will fit through the beds comfortably. Set the rose bushes far enough back from the edge of the beds so they do not entangle visitors (two feet is a good rule of thumb for most roses). Within the beds, rose plants are displayed most effectively when they are staggered within the rows, rather than lined up straight like a rank of toy soldiers.

Sit back on your terrace, relax, and enjoy the sight and fragrance of luminescent pink Electron and golden El Dorado.

Plant hybrid teas, like Secret Love, along a walk or drive, and enjoy the individual flowers as you stroll by each day.

Movable Roses

Rose gardening using containers reflects the movable and changeable ways and whims of today's society. Portable rose planters are not only a decorative addition to any part of the outdoor living area, they are also a perfect way to change the look of the landscape as quickly as you change your mind.

Movable roses extend the scope and possibilities for gardening spots. Wide paths and walkways can be highlighted with tubs of roses spotted here and there along them. If you have steps leading up to the front or back door, place a pot of roses on each tread to bring it to life.

Dress up windows with boxes of miniature roses. Rather than plant the roses directly into a soil-filled window box, fill the box with individual flower pots of minis. In that way, the roses can be easily moved indoors in winter or replaced quickly if something goes awry.

Patios, decks, and terraces have become favorite spots for entertaining and relaxing on warm summer days and evenings. Add to the pleasure of these moments with planters teeming with the color and fragrance of roses, such as the bicolor Snowfire and the orange-red Gypsy, *right.* Or let containers dress up a porch.

Brick or paved areas around swimming pools are often filled with lounge chairs and tables—but no color. Bring beauty right down to the water's edge with container planters of your favorite roses.

If you have a spot to hang a basket, fill it with miniature roses for a continuous display of summer color (and then move the basket indoors for the winter). The best varieties for baskets are Red Cascade, Green Ice, and Sugar Elf. Let their flowers cascade from lamp posts, tree limbs, gutters, overhangs, and brackets attached to fences or house.

If you have the space, grow movable roses in an out-of-the way place.

Should the plants in your containers lose their bloom or look less than ideal, they may easily be replaced by these fresher ones held in reserve.

Garden without a garden? Container plantings make it possible to grow roses on balconies, terraces, and roof tops high above city streets. The limited gardening space that comes with so many brownstones and town houses can be multiplied with portable planters.

Movable roses should be limited to shorter hybrid teas, floribundas, polyanthas, and miniatures. When planted in pots, these more compact roses look better than the tall hybrid tea or grandiflora. Shorter varieties produce flowers below eye level in height. Besides, the flowers on most of these roses appear in clusters, thereby covering the plant with more color at one time.

Tree roses, whether full size or miniature, are perfect choices for containers and should be placed wherever an accent is needed. Plant colorful geraniums or other annuals at the base of the tree rose to fill in the void and create two levels of interest.

Containers can be round, square, or any other shape so long as they are at least 18 inches across and deep. They can be made of plastic, clay, terra-cotta, ceramic, or one of the decay-resistant woods, like redwood, cypress, or cedar. And because they may be heavy and hard to move about, mount them on casters or on a dolly.

Although all roses, even those in containers, need at least six hours of sun a day, place movable roses in a spot where they receive morning sun

and some protection from the heat of the midday rays. Also try to keep them out of drying winds. Because the containers are exposed on all sides, they will dry more rapidly if overexposed to sun and wind. If roses in planters receive uneven sun and start growing in one direction to reach the light, be sure to rotate them every few days so they will grow straight.

Roses in containers need more watering than the same roses in the ground do. Not only are all sides of the container subject to drying wind and heat, there is also no ground moisture for the roots to rely on. So watch planters carefully, and water when the medium starts to dry out, never letting it become bone dry. Water until moisture runs from the bottom of the container. A mulch at the top of the planter will help keep the roses moist.

Planting medium for containers must be rich and well-drained. One of the packaged soilless potting mixes may be used, or mix your own soil, using equal parts of garden loam, sand, and peat moss or vermiculite. The high humus content will help to keep the medium moist.

The best fertilizer for movable roses is water soluble. Feed once a month, following label directions, or, for more even growth, every other week at half strength.

When winter comes, move the planters indoors (often impractical) or into an unheated porch, garage, or basement. The containers may also be sunk into the ground or placed in a cold frame. Check now and again to be sure the medium is slightly moist. If you choose to sink the planters in the ground, always add winter protection as suggested for garden-grown roses. See page 81. Then, in the early spring remove the planters from the ground, and place them in their previous locations. Prune away any winter-killed branches.

Movable Roses

Miniature roses are versatile movable plants, happy to spend the winter indoors after vacationing outside all summer. They can also be grown indoors all year or brought to life outdoors in summer and allowed to go dormant when cold weather comes.

Inside, minis need a lot of light, so grow them in an unobstructed south window or under ten to 14 hours of high-intensity, fluorescent lights per day. They thrive at normal household temperatures but like more humidity than most homes offer when the heat is on. To remedy this, grow minis on trays of pebbles, or mist them only on the morning of sunny days to limit the possibility of disease.

Indoors, the best planting medium for minis is a soilless mix of peat moss and perlite or vermiculite, although the same mixture used for outdoor movable roses can also be used with good success inside.

Miniature roses are thirsty plants and must be watered frequently enough to keep the medium evenly moist, neither soggy but not bone dry. Plastic pots are best for miniatures indoors because they don't dry out as quickly as clay pots do.

Start new miniature rose plants in four-inch pots, gradually working them into larger pots as they grow. One mini will fill out a small hanging basket, but for the ten- or 12-inch hanger, three plants are needed so the basket doesn't look skimpy.

Let fresh air reach your indoor miniature roses, but keep them out of cold drafts. Don't let the pots or plants touch each other; it will hamper air circulation and invite disease problems.

The major enemy of the miniature rose indoors is the spider mite; the best preventive and cure for this pest is water. Once a week, hold your plants upside down at the kitchen sink and spray away your problems with a stream of water. If mites should get away, spray the plants with water every day for ten days, or dip them into a warm detergent solution and rinse. Don't spray pesticides inside.

Fertilize movable roses indoors with a soluble plant food just as you would fertilize outdoor container plantings of roses.

You don't need to talk or sing to your miniature roses indoors, but they do benefit from being picked up every day. You can tell when they need watering and will be able to spot any troubles at the outset. Turn them around every so often so light strikes them evenly and they grow straight and uniformly. Pruning becomes an easy task if you regularly cut flowers for bouquets and boutonnieres.

Movable roses outdoors are cared for in the same way as roses planted into the garden, except for the differences already mentioned. Because they are planted in "up close" spots, they should always be picture perfect and may need a little extra attention. If you have an out-of-the-way garden corner, be sure to keep a few rose bushes growing in reserve to take over for any that aren't in peak bloom. In some ways, care of portable roses is easier because you can get to all sides of the plants to prune, spray, disbud, or cut flowers without becoming entangled in other bushes. Move the containers out of their spots for maintenance, and then move them back into place when finished. It's easy!

Enjoy the fragrant flowers of Mr. Lincoln, a popular hybrid tea.

Rev up an entry planting of evergreens and ground covers with a container of the low-growing floribunda, Puerto Rico.

Companions for Roses

If you want to show off your roses, don't let them stand alone. Giving them companions in the garden will complement and emphasize their beauty and charm.

Rose beds don't have to be unattractive expanses of bare ground and canes during the winter and early spring. Perk them up with colorful borders of snowdrops, crocus, squill, chionodoxa, and species tulips. Between the plants, clumps of golden daffodils glisten in the sunshine as the new foliage opens into bronze tones. By the time these bulbs have finished and the foliage disappears, the roses are ready to take over the limelight. As an added plus, fertilized roses will make the bulb flowers extraordinarily large.

Scads of spring perennials bloom before the roses. Use these freely without being concerned with color clash or interference. Try alyssum, creeping phlox, anemones, candytuft, or primroses for low-growing edgings to the rose border. Many of these will remain neat and attractive even when not in bloom.

Once roses come into bloom, they can rub shoulders with all sorts of other plants and together earn their place in the sun. These plants will provide color should the roses be between blooming periods. Choose the companions carefully, and practice a little caution when deciding on colors and sizes. They should complement the beauty of the roses but not dominate the scene.

Companion plants to roses in beds will most likely be used as borders and interplantings. Most low-growing annuals fill this role perfectly and do not compete for water and food, as do the heavy-rooted perennials.

Color is not the beginning and end of gardening, but it is used to create accent, emphasis, balance, and rhythm and is important in the selection of companions for roses.

Blue is a popular companion color because there are no blue roses. The deep blues of cornflower, anchusa, and clematis blend beautifully with soft yellow and red roses. White, orange, and pale pink roses can be used with the clear blue of delphinium. Veronica, asters, bellflower, verbena, and petunias are also good sources of blue contrast —just don't try to mix them with most mauve roses which will look washed out in comparison.

Red as a color in the garden is too much if it predominates, but it shouldn't be omitted either. For attention and accent, red can't be beat, but use it discreetly. Red companions go best with white, soft yellow, or clear-pink roses. Annual phlox, verbena, aster, balsam, petunias, and portulaca all have red flowering forms.

Orange companions bring brilliance and warmth to roses and are used most effectively with dark red, yellow, or pure white roses. Gazania, portulaca, marigolds, calendula, and lantana are good orange choices; but they'll clash with pink rose petals.

Yellow is the light and life of the garden, always adding a touch of gaiety to the scene. Deep yellow roses are intensified with a light, almost cream-colored zinnia. The yellow of celosia, sanvitalia, or linum brings a harmonious accent to orange, red, pink, mauve, or white roses. Yellow will make delicate shades sparkle and add warmth and cheer to darker roses. Use it thoughtfully, trying, in most settings, to match pale with pale and strong with strong.

Pink is a color that, used in the garden alone, is not strong enough unless varying shades of it are combined (right). Many pink flowers are beautiful in plantings of roses with contrasting tones. Pink geraniums appear even pinker next to white roses. Clear pink is striking next to mauve roses and red ones, too, if the hue is just right. Harmonize pale yellow roses and yellow blends with pink snapdragons, or bring pink to the garden with sweet william, verbena, or petunias.

Though you might think it is, white isn't always easy to use in the garden. White is often used as a foil between two strong colors. No problem, so long as it does not disturb the unity of the scheme. But too much of it will make the garden seem spotty. Bold masses of white produce a dignity hard to beat. Interspersed with strong colors, white softens; used among paler tints, it strengthens.

White flowers come from many sources—begonias, sweet alyssum, portulaca, balsam, or geraniums. They can be combined with nearly every rose.

Violet is often difficult to use effectively in the garden. Deep shades will stand out against mauve roses and blend well with pink roses so long as they do not have much red in them. Violet also is very attractive with soft yellow; with white, it brings a pleasant, cooling effect. Think twice before combining violet with roses of red, orange, or strong yellow. Violet, purple, and magenta tones are found in asters, sweet alyssum, heliotrope, nierembergia, or verbena.

Don't think of flower color only when choosing companions for roses. Plants with silver or gray leaves add a charm independent of their blossoms and, while lightening heavy colors, bring conflicting colors into a pleasing relationship. Good choices include dusty miller (centaurea) and either Silver King or Silver Mound artemesia.

Companions for Roses

Roses should be thought of as perennials and combined with them in planting beds. Golden coreopsis and daylilies are striking next to the hot orange of Tropicana or Fragrant Cloud. After they bloom, the flowers of yarrow leave behind delicate, fernlike foliage. The burst of color with which roses herald the beginning of fall is heightened by chrysanthemums.

A touch of white for here and there in the perennial rose bed is achieved easily with shasta daisy or phlox, plants that also will benefit from exposure to the sun. If you want blue, interplant roses with scabiosa, delphinium, cornflower, bellflower, aster, anchusa, balloon flower, flax, or nierembergia.

Lilies are perfect companions for roses, they like the same growing conditions and, with proper selection, will bloom all summer in many complementary colors. Don't forget the other bulbs, especially the tender ones, to fill in spots of color among the roses. Gladiolus, dahlias, canna lilies, freesia, and many others are perfect for instant companionship and for filling in unsightly bare spaces in the garden. If the soil beneath your roses is cool and shady, try a mass planting of tuberous begonias.

Geraniums, too, will find a place wherever roses grow. Should a favorite rose not survive the winter, its spot can quickly be filled in with pink, red, or white from these common garden favorites.

Roses that climb on trellises or against houses should have annual or perennial plants below them. Vines such as clematis look and perform better with a rose bush set in front of their base. Roses are also a good choice in front of other climbers such as thunbergia, morning glory, or Dutchman's pipe.

Tall growers used for the back of the border, such as delphinium, hollyhock, or cosmos, will stand out even more with roses of contrasting colors set in front of them. Miniature

Marigolds reflect colors of Lemon Spice and Seventh Heaven.

roses or ground-hugging annuals can blanket the area between and in front of the roses. They will also help keep weed growth choked out.

Instead of planting roses in containers to add interest to flower and shrub beds, try the opposite. Portable planters of marigolds, zinnias, geraniums, petunias, or annual phlox can add a contrast in color and texture to rose beds. If your roses are near the house or patio, dress the sky above them by hanging baskets of annuals from nearby posts and overhangs. These containers, strategically placed, not only lend a colorful touch, they also create a line leading the eye to the focal point of the garden, the rose bed.

Companions for roses don't have to be alive. If you have a red climber on a fence, give it a coat of white paint to create a dazzling effect. If the climber is a softer tone of pastel pink, yellow, or apricot, a naturally weathered, gray split-rail fence provides a subtle combination.

A statue, sundial, bird bath, garden light, small pool—these are only a few of the items that when combined with roses make interesting garden features.

Bermudiana's two-toned buds open to a pleasing clear pink, combining with the blue of Belladonna delphiniums.

Companions for Roses

Edgings of white alyssum complement dazzling Sunsprite.

Companions for roses need not be limited to flowering annuals, bulbs, or perennials; shrubs also make good neighbors. Use roses with shrubs in two different ways: to extend the blooming period of spring-flowering forsythia, spirea, azaleas, lilacs, viburnum, or beauty bush, or to provide a colorful complement for summer-flowering shrubs. For beds of this type, plant weigela, mock orange, abelia, rose of sharon, vitex, or hydrangea.

A small, decorative tree is a lovely companion for the rose garden. In spring, blooms from cherry trees, magnolia, dogwood, flowering peach, crab apple, or hawthorn fill the air before the roses show off theirs. Later on, the tree provides a pretty place to rest under. Place the tree so the roses are in its shade during the afternoon, and put a bench under it so you can sit and enjoy the rose garden. Don't plant the roses too close to the tree, or they will fight for sun, food, and water.

Let's go one step further. Don't think ornamentals are the only companions for roses. Think of planting edibles, too, in rose and mixed flower beds.

Vegetable gardens are usually put off by themselves, and they shouldn't be. Many edibles are attractive. They can easily mix with roses, and they love the same things roses do—sun, food, rich soil, and water. Roses can be planted in front of trellises bearing cucumbers, beans, or squash; they can go between tomatoes and peppers. To save space, grow underground crops such as beets, carrots, and onions between the rose bushes. To edge rose beds, try sage, thyme, or parsley.

The one thing you must watch when mixing roses and edibles is the use of pesticides. Read labels carefully to make sure the material is suitable for crops and to find out how long you must wait between spraying and harvesting. Many of the commonly sold rose pesticides are harmful to vegetable crops.

COMBINATIONS TO TRY

With red roses . . .
Yellow portulaca
Pink wax begonias
Dwarf white snapdragons
Peter Pan Orange zinnia
Amethyst verbena

With pink roses . . .
Blue salvia
Dwarf coreopsis
Sprinter Scarlet geranium
Rosie O'Day sweet alyssum
White Cascade petunia

With orange roses . . .
Showboat marigold
Crystal Palace lobelia
Dwarf calliopsis
Silver dusty miller
White gypsophila
Canary Bird zinnia

With yellow roses . . .
Pink Beauty phlox
White TomThumb balsam
Purple Robe nierembergia
Petite Orange marigold
Old Mexico zinnia
Blue Blazer ageratum

With white roses . . .
Baby blue eyes
Saint John's Fire salvia
Gaillardia Lollipop
Pacific Beauty calendula
Blue Picotee petunia

With mauve roses . . .
Yellow dwarf dahlias
Gray santolina
Pink bachelor buttons
Snowflake dianthus
Blushing Maid petunia

The royal color of violas strikingly contrasts with the subtle pink of Gay Princess.

Color Schemes

There are those who think shades of color will not clash naturally. They plant their gardens in every color of the rainbow. But unfortunately, the beauty of many subtle tones is lost in the confusion. The proper color scheme will bring out the best of everything.

Monochromatic color schemes may be dull and uninteresting; those using a dominant color with a contrasting secondary color are more striking. The lesser color will not compete with the main one but instead will accentuate it. If you like yellow, roses in various shades of gold will dominate, tied together by blue, orange, scarlet, or pink.

Another color scheme uses two dominant colors, softened by a touch here and there of a third. Deliberately putting two strongly contrasting colors together creates drama in the garden. Look at Heat Wave and Pascali, *right*.

Another principle allows for many colors in a logical gradation or progression; they can be pale to dark or a central focus of strong colors leading through transitional shades to lighter tones. The many different colors can be unified with a border of white or soft pastel.

Designing the garden is not the same as flower arranging or interior decorating, because you must take into consideration the effects of sunlight and the competitive contrast of a green landscape and blue sky. The principles of color harmony have less impact in the great outdoors where weather conditions play more of a modifying role.

Look to nature, however, for ideas on color schemes for roses. She combines some opposite hues in a startling manner. There are daisies of pink and white, violet asters with yellow centers, red and yellow gaillardia, marigolds of orange and gold, red and white impatiens, or red and pink phlox. Borrow from these natural palettes to get ideas for the rose bed.

When planning the garden, remember that solid colors are more difficult to harmonize than blends. They have no contrasts on their flowers, no tones to be picked up by a neighbor. On the other hand, put too many blends together and the delicacy of their subtle colors will be lost. Following the same theory, too many pinks together will wash each other out. A good rule of thumb is to place blends next to solids to make the better qualities of each stand out. Light-colored blends are easy to mix with most any color.

ROSE COMBINATIONS

Garden Party and Electron
Rose Parade and Oregold
Spanish Sun and Angel Face
Duet and Lady X
Tiffany and Lemon Spice
Neue Revue and Red Lion
Ivory Fashion and Peer Gynt
Anabell and Irish Gold
Europeana and Bahia
Royal Highness and Christian Dior
Gene Boerner and Apricot Nectar
Fragrant Cloud and Saratoga
Sunsprite and Accent
Iceberg and Sundowner
Chrysler Imperial and King's Ransom
Peace and Pink Peace
Orangeade and Sarabande

Matador and Summer Sunshine
Mister Lincoln and Pascali
Fire King and Woburn Abbey
Pristine and Granada
Seashell and First Edition
Evening Star and Heirloom
Queen Elizabeth and Susan Massu
Red Masterpiece and Paradise
Portrait and Mt. Shasta
Chicago Peace and Promise
Mojave and American Heritage
Big Ben and Century Two
Prominent and Redgold
Medallion and Matterhorn
Blue Moon and Michele Meilland
Double Delight and White Masterpiece
Sunset Jubilee and Portrait

Color Schemes

Another difference between flower arranging and choosing a color scheme for the garden is that you have to make your plans without having the flower to look at. This requires early planning, a good memory, or good notes. As you see something you like in a friend's or public garden, jot down the name and the color. It will make things easier later on.

Use color to provide accent. Relieve large masses of one color with a smaller group of plants of a complementary color—or by the sparing introduction of white. Color accents along a border produce movement, rhythm, and sequence. They carry the eye along to the climactic point.

Climax is important for every garden, no matter what the size. The point of climax should be stressed in the design, and the roses with the strongest colors should be placed near this focal point.

Placement of color is also very important in the scheme of things. Don't concentrate the color of roses in one bed and not use it elsewhere. Spread color all about the garden to create the illusion of abundance. Correct placement of colorful roses will also lead the eye away from unattractive eyesores.

Choice of color is vital. Warm-toned roses in shades of red, yellow, or orange convey boldness and make the garden appear smaller. White and mauve roses give a cool feeling and make the garden seem larger. Rarely, however, is limiting the garden to either warm or cool roses an effective technique. Both should be used, and each will help the other.

The color scheme you choose for your garden may also depend on whether you're a man or a woman. In the past, some men seem to prefer the strong reds and oranges while women often favored the pastels.

However, this tradition shouldn't limit you in choosing colors for your garden. Today's trend is definitely a bold one. Contemporary gardeners crave color in large masses and in forceful combinations. Don't be afraid to put strong contrasts together, and use the easy-to-mix creams, buffs, light yellows, and pink and yellow blends to buffer strong colors and tie the color scheme of the garden together.

The most effective way to use the colors you choose is to plant them in masses. Whether it be a dominant color scheme or one using two or three colors, it is a much more forceful technique to have the colors in blocks, rather than scattered about like a checkerboard. To achieve this, at least two and preferably three of a variety should be planted together. This goes for the annual or perennial companions as well as the roses. Drifts of individual complementary colors are far more effective than a crazy-quilt pattern of scattered colors.

One final but important considera-

Lavender Angel Face with White Knight has a timeless quality.

tion in choosing a color scheme is taking a hard look at what is already there. What color is the house? The fence? The driveway? The deck? Unless you are willing to change the color or buy something new, you will have to work your color scheme around what you already have. This background color is so obvious it is often overlooked, but it shouldn't be because it can mean the difference between a spectacular garden and a lackluster one.

If the house is green or one of the earth tones, any color scheme will do. After all, these are the colors of nature. Against a red house, concentrate yellow or white; a blue house looks special with plantings of red, pink, white, or yellow. If the house is yellow or gold, try orange or pink. White on white can be sterile, but with the right accents, the combination can be breath-taking.

No one can tell you what color scheme you should be using. Only suggestions and guidelines can be given. Response to color is a very private thing, a reflection of the personality. Some people prefer the warm tones; others are lovers of cool colors. Taste is as different as night and day, as black and white. Only a purist will plant only one color in his or her garden. As for you, it's your garden. You decide.

The deep, velvety red of Proud Land forms a stunning partnership in the garden with the pinks and coral of Vin Rose.

ALL-AMERICA ROSE SELECTIONS

In 1938, rose producers and introducers banded together and formed the All-America Rose Selections (AARS). This organization was set up to test new roses and determine which, if any, were worthy of recommendation to the buying public.

Plants are grown in 26 test gardens across the United States and Canada so that each rose tested is exposed to a variety of soil and climatic conditions. They are rated on habit, vigor, hardiness, disease resistance, repeat bloom, foliage, form, substance, opening and finishing color, fragrance, and novelty. After a two-year test, those rose varieties with the highest scores are awarded the green and white AARS stamp. They are then released for sale to the public.

Year	Award Winner	Color	Class	Originator
1979	Friendship	Pink	Hybrid tea	Robert Lindquist Sr.
	Paradise	Lavender and pink	Hybrid tea	O. L. Weeks
	Sundowner	Orange	Grandiflora	Sam McGredy IV
1978	Charisma	Multicolor red/yellow	Floribunda	Robert Jelly
	Color Magic	Coral blend	Hybrid tea	Wm. Warriner
1977	Double Delight	Red and white bicolor	Hybrid tea	H. C. Swim
	First Edition	Coral	Floribunda	Georges Delbard
	Prominent	Hot orange	Grandiflora	Reimer Kordes
1976	America	Salmon	Climber	Wm. Warriner
	Cathedral	Golden apricot	Floribunda	Sam McGredy IV
	Seashell	Peach & salmon	Hybrid tea	Reimer Kordes
	Yankee Doodle	Sherbet orange	Hybrid tea	Reimer Kordes
1975	Arizona	Bronze-copper	Grandiflora	O. O. Weeks
	Oregold	Pure yellow	Hybrid tea	Matthias Tantau
	Rose Parade	Pink	Floribunda	J. Benjamin Williams
1974	Bahia	Orange-pink	Floribunda	Lammerts
	Bon Bon	Pink and white bicolor	Floribunda	Warriner
	Perfume Delight	Clear pink	Hybrid tea	Weeks
1973	Electron	Rose-pink	Hybrid tea	Sam McGredy IV
	Gypsy	Orange-red	Hybrid tea	O. L. Weeks
	Medallion	Apricot-pink	Hybrid tea	Wm. Warriner
1972	Apollo	Sunrise yellow	Hybrid tea	D. L. Armstrong
	Portrait	Pink	Hybrid tea	Carl Meyer
1971	Aquarius	Pink blend	Grandiflora	D. L. Armstrong
	Command Performance	Orange-red	Hybrid tea	Lindquist
	Redgold	Red edge on yellow	Floribunda	Dickson
1970	First Prize	Rose-red	Hybrid tea	Boerner
1969	Angel Face	Lavender	Floribunda	Swim & Weeks
	Comanche	Scarlet-orange	Grandiflora	Swim & Weeks
	Gene Boerner	Pink	Floribunda	Boerner
	Pascali	White	Hybrid tea	Louis Lens
1968	Europeana	Red	Floribunda	G. deRuiter
	Miss All-American Beauty	Pink	Hybrid tea	Meilland
	Scarlet Knight	Scarlet red	Grandiflora	Meilland
1967	Bewitched	Clear, phlox-pink	Hybrid tea	Lammerts
	Gay Princess	Shell pink	Floribunda	Boerner
	Lucky Lady	Creamy, shrimp-pink	Grandiflora	D. L. Armstrong & Swim
	Roman Holiday	Orange-red	Floribunda	Lindquist

Year	Award Winner	Color	Class	Originator
1966	American Heritage	Ivory tinged carmine	Hybrid tea	Lammerts
	Apricot Nectar	Apricot	Floribunda	Boerner
	Matterhorn	White	Hybrid tea	D. L. Armstrong & Swim
1965	Camelot	Shrimp pink	Grandiflora	Swim & Weeks
	Mister Lincoln	Deep red	Hybrid tea	Swim & Weeks
1964	Granada	Scarlet-yellow	Hybrid tea	Lindquist
	Saratoga	White	Floribunda	Boerner
1963	Royal Highness	Clear pink	Hybrid tea	Swim & Weeks
	Tropicana	Orange-red	Hybrid tea	Matthias Tantau
1962	Christian Dior	Crimson-scarlet	Hybrid tea	F. Meilland
	Golden Slippers	Orange-gold	Floribunda	Von Abrams
	John S. Armstrong	Deep red	Grandiflora	Swim
	King's Ransom	Chrime yellow	Hybrid tea	Morey
1961	Duet	Salmon-pink, orange-red	Hybrid tea	Swim
	Pink Parfait	Dawn pink	Grandiflora	Swim
1960	Fire King	Vermillion	Floribunda	F. Meilland
	Garden Party	White	Hybrid tea	Swim
	Sarabande	Scarlet orange	Floribunda	F. Meilland
1959	Ivory Fashion	Ivory	Floribunda	Boerner
	Starfire	Cherry red	Grandiflora	Lammerts
1958	Fusilier	Orange-red	Floribunda	Morey
	Gold Cup	Golden yellow	Floribunda	Boerner
	White Knight	White	Hybrid tea	F. Meilland
1957	Golden Showers	Daffodil yellow	Climber	Lammerts
	White Bouquet	White	Floribunda	Boerner
1956	Circus	Multicolor	Floribunda	Swim
1955	Jiminy Cricket	Coral orange	Floribunda	Boerner
	Queen Elizabeth	Clear pink	Grandiflora	Lammerts
	Tiffany	Orchid pink	Hybrid tea	Lindquist
1954	*Lilibet	Dawn pink	Floribunda	Lindquist
	Mojave	Apricot orange	Hybrid tea	Swim
1953	Chrysler Imperial	Crimson red	Hybrid tea	Lammerts
	Ma Perkins	Coral-shell pink	Floribunda	Boerner
1952	*Fred Howard	Yellow, penciled pink	Hybrid tea	F. H. Howard
	Helen Traubel	Apricot pink	Hybrid tea	Swim
	Vogue	Cherry coral	Floribunda	Boerner
1951	None of the 1951 introductions was equal to the rigid AARS standards.			
1950	Capistrano	Pink	Hybrid tea	Morris
	Fashion	Coral pink	Floribunda	Boerner
	Sutter's Gold	Golden yellow	Hybrid tea	Swim
1949	Forty-niner	Red and yellow	Hybrid tea	Swim
	*Tallyho	Two-tone pink	Hybrid tea	Swim
1948	Diamond Jubilee	Buff	Hybrid tea	Boerner
	Nocturne	Dark red	Hybrid tea	Swim
	Pinkie	Light rose pink	Floribunda	Swim
	Taffeta	Carmine	Hybrid tea	Lammerts
1947	Rubaiyat	Cerise red	Hybrid tea	McGredy
1946	Peace	Pale gold	Hybrid tea	F. Meilland

No longer generally available.

ROSE FAVORITES

The American Rose Society, a national association of amateur and professional rose growers, has categorized all old garden, shrub, hybrid tea, floribunda, grandiflora, polyantha, climbing, and miniature roses into sixteen separate color classifications. This list of classifications makes the job of picking the best roses a lot easier.

w—white or near white
my—medium yellow
dy—deep yellow
yb—yellow blend
ab—apricot blend
ob—orange and orange
    blend
o-r—orange-red

lp—light pink
mp—medium pink
pb—pink blend
mr—medium red
dr—dark red
rb—red blend
m—mauve
r—russet

Each year, members of the American Rose Society are surveyed to establish ratings for the varieties grown across the country. The rating system is based on a ten-point scale.

10.0 Perfect (never achieved)
9.0-9.9 Outstanding
8.0-8.9 Excellent
7.0-7.9 Good
6.0-6.9 Fair
5.9 and lower (of questionable value)

The results of this annual survey are published in the "Handbook for Selecting Roses," available from the American Rose Society for 25 cents. Write to Box 30,000, Shreveport, Louisiana 71130. It lists over 1,000 different rose varieties. The roses listed here have all attained a rating of 8.0 or higher.

HYBRID TEAS

White
Garden Party w
Pascali w

Yellow
Peace yb
Susan Massu yb

Orange
Fragrant Cloud o-r
Tropicana o-r

Pink
Century Two mp
Chicago Peace pb
Confidence pb
Dainty Bess lp
Duet mp
First Prize pb
Miss All-American Beauty mp
Royal Highness lp
Swarthmore pb
Tiffany pb

Red
Big Ben dr
Chrysler Imperial dr
Double Delight rb
Granada rb
Mister Lincoln dr
Wini Edmunds rb

Mauve
Lady X m

GRANDIFLORAS

Pink
Pink Parfait pb
Queen Elizabeth mp

FLORIBUNDAS

White
Evening Star w
Iceberg w
Ivory Fashion w

Yellow
Little Darling yb

Orange
Bahia ob
City of Belfast o-r
Ginger o-r
Matador ob
Orangeade o-r
Sarabande o-r

Pink
Betty Prior mp
Gene Boerner mp
Sea Pearl pb
Red Europeana dr

Mauve
Angel Face m

POLYANTHA

Pink
The Fairy lp

CLIMBERS

Apricot
Royal Sunset ab

Pink
Climbing First Prize pb

Red
Don Juan dr
Handel rb

MINIATURES

White
Cinderella w
Easter Morning w
Popcorn w
Simplex w
Starglo w

Yellow
Yellow Doll my

Apricot
Baby Darling ab
Mary Adair ab

Orange
Hula Girl ob
Mary Marshall ob
Scarlet Gen o-r
Sheri Anne o-r
Starina o-r

Pink
Baby Betsy McCall lp
Chipper lp
Hi Ho dp
Janna pb
Jeanne Lajoie mp
Judy Fischer mp
Kathy Robinson pb
Pink Cameo dp
Pixie Rose dp

Red
Beauty Secret mr
Dwarfking mr
Jeanie Williams rb
Kathy mr
Magic Carrousel rb
Over the Rainbow rb
Top Secret mr

Bahia shows its prizewinning style with exuberant displays of ruffled, orange-red flowers.

A Rose is a Rose
Is a
Rose

Shakespeare once wrote that a rose by any other name was still a rose and smelled as sweet. Whether they're fragrant or not, roses come in sizes, forms, and colors to win any heart. Choosing roses is as easy as A,B,C — alba, bourbon, centifolia, damask, eglanteria, floribunda, grandiflora, hybrid tea. . . .

When you plant roses, you plant for years of beauty. To make sure you achieve it, plan ahead; later you can sit back and enjoy the garden. Choose your roses with care, looking at color, form, height, and hardiness before buying. With success come satisfaction, happiness, admiration.

Old Garden Roses

It's more than nostalgia or historical significance that makes all of the roses in grandmother's garden so popular. They stand on their own virtues—beauty, fragrance, hardiness, low maintenance, charm, long life. Flowers of all colors vary in form—from delicate singles to robust doubles. Old garden roses are a welcome contrast to the styles of today, a not-to-be-forgotten link with yesterday. By definition, any rose belonging to a class in existence before hybrid teas (1867) is an old garden rose.

ALBA

Albas are tall, dense, hardy, and disease-resistant roses characterized by blue-green foliage. Medium-size flowers are in tones of pink or white, borne in clusters and deliciously fragrant. Like so many of the old fashioned roses, they bloom only once a year.

KÖNIGIN von DÄNEMARK
Flesh pink, very double, quartered flowers have a darker center and unfold from a peachy bud.

MAIDEN'S BLUSH
Blush pink, globular flowers fading to white bloom on long arching canes.

BOURBON

Vigorous, shrubby plants have glossy, bright green leaves and clusters of fragrant double flowers. Bourbons are moderately hardy and exhibit good repeat bloom.

LA REINE VICTORIA
This slender, upright rose has cup-shaped, rich pink flowers that deepen in tone with age. Its famous sport, Mme. Pierre Oger, is identical in all respects, except the flower is blush pink, developing a rosy cast as it opens. Both varieties are hardy and relatively disease resistant. The flowers are deeply fragrant and long lasting when cut.

SOUVENIR de la MALMAISON
Large, flat, quartered blooms of flesh pink with a rosy center appear freely on a dwarf, compact plant.

VARIEGATA di BOLOGNA
One of the finest striped roses. This tall-growing plant has globular white flowers, striped in purplish-red shades.

CENTIFOLIA

These are the cabbage roses, so named for the 100 or more petals that overlap like leaves of a cabbage. They are also called Provence roses for the part of France where they were once widely grown. Globular flowers of white through deep rose bloom once a year on slender, arching branches that carry wrinkled leaves. The blooms have a sweet fragrance; the plants are very hardy.

PETITE de HOLLANDE
Small, double, rose-pink flowers bloom in clusters on a medium-size, bushy plant.

ROSE de MEAUX
This is the miniature of the old garden roses. Tiny, double, light pink flowers are like pompons and give a charming, airy grace to this short plant. Although hardy in most areas of the country, this variety is susceptible to black spot disease. Flowers are about 1½ inches wide and come in either red or white. Plants will grow 2 feet tall.

CHINA

The Chinas, with delicate-textured small flowers of pink or red, have played an important role in the development of modern roses. Their reliable and consistent repeat bloom coupled with glossy, almost evergreen foliage is a definite plus; unfortunately, they are extremely tender.

GREEN ROSE
An oddity in the rose world is the green rose, *Rosa chinensis viridiflora*. The flowers are very small; the green "petals" are actually a multitude of sepals.

HERMOSA
High-centered, fragrant, double, blush-pink flowers that bloom in clusters are set off by blue-green leaves.

OLD BLUSH
Two-tone pink, semi-double flowers appear in large clusters on an upright plant and have only a slight fragrance.

DAMASK

Known for their fragrance, these roses are medium to large in size, with drooping or arching branches. They're extremely hardy and disease resistant. Except for the autumn damasks, they bloom just once.

CELSIANA
A graceful, slender plant with gray-toned foliage bears large, semi-double blooms of pale pink that fade to a warm blush. The petals are crinkled, giving an interesting appearance to the flower. Gold stamens set off the center of the flower. The loose, informal flowers are flat and once blooming.

MADAM HARDY
One of the most splendid white roses of all time is this very double, cup-shaped flower that opens flat to reveal a green eye in the center. A tinge of pink often appears on the buds of these spring bloomers.

ROSE de RESCHT
Rosettes of bright fuchsia to deep pink flowers bloom over a long season on dwarf, compact bushes.

GALLICA

The French rose, and the oldest one known, has flowers of red, pink, or purple over dark green, rough-textured leaves. The plants are hardy but occasionally will look spindly; the flowers may be single or double, with tremendous fragrance or none at all, and bloom once in spring.

CAMAIEUX
Low-growing plants have semi-double flowers of white, striped with rosy purple; they have a spicy fragrance.

CARDINAL de RICHELIEU
Dark, wine-red to purple flowers are large, fragrant, and double. The bush is medium in height and about as wide as tall.

CHARLES de MILLS

Rounded, cup-shaped blooms packed with petals give this variety an almost crepe paper-like appearance. Flowers are deep red with purplish undertone. A very popular and vigorous variety.

ROSA MUNDI
This rose, known botanically as *Rosa gallica versicolor*, is striped pink, red, and white, every petal different from the other. The flowers are semi-double and accented with bright yellow stamens. It is often confused with York and Lancaster.

HYBRID FOETIDA

This class of roses contributed its beautiful yellow color to modern hybrids. The plants are vigorous, tall, once blooming, but susceptible to black spot. The name comes from the offensive odor found in the species.

HARISON'S YELLOW

Clouds of small, semi-double, open, very fragrant, bright yellow flowers cover this plant and almost hide its small, rich green, ferny leaves. Early American settlers took this rose with them wherever they went.

HYBRID PERPETUAL

This class is the transition between old and modern roses. The plants are tall, vigorous, hardy, and bloom repeatedly all summer. Flowers are large, double, and colored white, pink, red, or mauve.

BARONESS ROTHSCHILD
Stiff, erect plants are graced with large, fully double, cupped flowers of soft rose, tinted with white.

FRAU KARL DRUSCHKI
Pointed buds open into sparkling snow white flowers, often touched with pink. It's one of the best. Plants easily grow six feet tall and flower repeatedly all season long.

GÉNERAL JACQUEMINOT
Long stems made this an early florist's rose. Blooms are cupped, bright, clear red, and distinctively fragrant.

MRS. JOHN LAING
Low-growing for its class, this rose is covered with soft pink flowers that are strongly fragrant.

PAUL NEYRON
Cupped flowers of rose-pink tinted lilac bloom on long stems over rich green foliage.

ROGER LAMBELIN
This rose is very distinct, with wavy petals of maroon, edged in white. A medium-size plant, its flower is slightly fragrant.

HYBRID SPINOSISSIMA

Hybrids of the Scotch rose are mostly modern additions to the shrub border, valued for their bloom.

FRÜHLINGSGOLD
Although it blooms only once, this rose is worth the space if you want a large, vigorous plant with arching canes filled with good-sized, single, very fragrant flowers of pure golden yellow.

STANWELL PERPETUAL
Blush-pink flowers are medium-size, sweetly fragrant, double, and repeat blooming on this large but graceful plant.

MOSS

Mutations of the centifolias, the moss roses have small, hairy glands covering the sepals (and sometimes the stem and leaves) that look like moss and produce a marvelous fragrance. The plants are hardy and, for the most part, medium in height, ranging from six to eight feet. The flowers are large, double, and globular, blooming later in the spring than most roses. Most varieties of moss roses bloom only once a year. Others will bloom sporadically throughout the summer and early fall.

ALFRED de DALMAS

Called Mousseline by some, this rose is a compact grower with pale pink flowers that bleach to white in the heat of the sun. It shows some repeat bloom.

COMMON MOSS
Globular flowers open flat to reveal a button center amid clear pink petals. This very popular moss rose is also called Communis.

CRESTED MOSS
Summer clusters of pink flowers open from tri-cornered, mossy buds, giving the rose its other name, Chapeau de Napoléon.

GLOIRE des MOUSSEUX
Midsummer blooms are a clear, bright salmon pink, deeper in the center and appearing in clusters.

SALET
Flowers of rosy pink open flat and show some repeat bloom.

NOISETTE

Mild-climate-only plants are tall, making good climbers, and bear clusters of white, red, pink, purple, or yellow flowers throughout summer.

MARECHAL NIEL
Large double flowers of golden yellow bloom profusely, with a strong fragrance.

PORTLAND

Sturdy, erect bushes produce double, very fragrant flowers all season.

JACQUES CARTIER
Light pink flowers with a dark button center are large and full, often quartered, blooming atop light green leaves. Not winter hardy.

SPECIES

Species roses are wild roses, but many deserve a place in the garden. All are single-flowered, and most grow into very large plants.

AUSTRIAN COPPER
Rosa foetida bicolor
Arching canes are smothered in late spring with masses of coppery-red flowers that are golden yellow on the reverse of the petals.

CHESTNUT ROSE
Rosa roxburghi
Gray branches shed their bark, and the flower bud looks like a chestnut burr, making this rose unique. The flowers are double, flat, and medium pink; the bush repeats its bloom and grows close to the ground.

FATHER HUGO'S ROSE
Rosa hugonis
This rose is one of the first to bloom and should be grown as a climber. The masses of flowers are sunny yellow, blooming on drooping branches over small, dark green leaves.

TEA

Translucent, pastel flowers that give color to the garden all summer also emit a delicious, fresh-tea-leaf fragrance. The teas are graceful but tender plants of medium height.

CATHERINE MERMET
Double flowers of soft flesh pink with lilac edges and creamy overtones have perfect form. The stems are long and perfect for cutting.

MAMAN COCHET
Very double, large flowers have classic form and petals of soft pink with a yellow base. Flowers are scented and appear all season long. It will grow four feet tall.

Shrub-Like Roses

So often and unjustifiably neglected in the landscape setting is the shrub rose. Few plants in a mixed border are so tough, hardy, and tolerant of neglect and poor growing conditions. Use shrub roses singly or in mass for a bold effect. They vary in height, from ground covers to hedges and screens, and bloom in all colors and flower forms for a longer period than any other shrub. Large yet luxuriant, the shrub rose, whether old fashioned or modern, deserves to be in every garden.

EGLANTERIA

Hybrids of the Sweetbrier rose have a large, dense, thorny habit of growth and leaves that are scented like apples. Small single or semi-double flowers of pink, red, copper, or yellow bloom in spring on hardy plants that will often grow from eight to 12 feet high. Colorful hips appear after each bloom.

LADY PENZANCE
Small, single flowers of coppery pink with yellow centers bloom on large, arching plants that look almost scarlet from a distance. Foliage and flowers are fragrant, but plants are susceptible to black spot.

LORD PENZANCE
Clusters of small fawn flowers, tinted lemon-yellow, bloom on strong stems. This variety does not bloom as early or as long as Lady Penzance.

HYBRID MOYESI

Hybrids of *Rosa moyesi* are large, stiff, hardy plants. Most will reach about six feet in height. All have uniquely attractive red hips following each bloom. Most are very disease resistant.

NEVADA
Pink buds open into creamy-white, large, single flowers that are often splashed with red. Each flower has attractive, prominent, golden-yellow stamens. The plant is vigorous and shows repeat bloom. Most will grow five to seven feet tall.

HYBRID RUGOSA

Hybrids of *Rosa rugosa* show the same characteristics as their parent—hardiness; disease resistance; easy care; large, dense growth; and deep green, wrinkled foliage. Their hips are a valued source of vitamin C.

BLANC DOUBLE de COUBERT

Large, double, very fragrant, snow-white blooms appear all summer on large, spreading plants that grow to five feet in height. Flowers are sweetly fragrant and are followed by attractive red hips in the fall. Mature hips are an excellent source of vitamin C. This variety is one of the best white shrubs.

DELICATA

This rose is anything but delicate. It will thrive where winter temperatures drop to 50 degrees below zero (Fahrenheit); it will do equally well on coastal sand dunes where the air is salt laden. The three-inch blooms appear repeatedly; hips are the size and color of crab apples, and they are high in vitamin C.

F. J. GROOTENDORST

Tiny, double flowers are frilled like carnations and bloom in clusters throughout the summer on tall, upright plants. Well-known sports of this rose include Pink Grootendorst, a medium dusty pink, and Grootendorst Supreme, a bright medium crimson, identical in all respects except for flower color. All three can reach six feet tall.

MAX GRAF

This rose is valuable as a ground cover or trailer. It has large, single, bright pink flowers with golden centers. Bloom is profuse and fragrant but appears only once per season. Good choice for problem slopes where other ground covers will not thrive.

KORDESI

These modern shrubs and semi-climbers are very hardy and offer a variety of flower forms and colors. All have glossy foliage.

DORTMUND

A vigorous climber, this rose has large, single, striking crimson flowers with white eyes. The blooms grow in clusters and repeat profusely. Bright orange hips form after flowers fade. This variety will eventually grow 15 feet long.

HEIDELBERG

Clusters of large, scarlet and crimson flowers bloom on a bushy plant. Use as either a shrub or climber.

MUSK

Musks, or hybrid moschatas, will grow in less sun than any other rose. They bloom all season in large clusters or trusses; their fragrance is heavy. Some varieties have double or semi-double flowers but most are singles. Plants are tall, disease resistant, and moderately hardy.

BELINDA

Wavy petals of soft pink grace semi-double, white-centered flowers. Plants flower repeatedly on trusses ten feet in length.

BUFF BEAUTY

A beauty it is, with double flowers of pale apricot-yellow. Plants grow six feet tall and are a good choice for planting along a fence.

CORNELIA

Coral-pink flowers are flushed with yellow and are small, double, and fluffy. Blooms appear all summer, even in partial shade. Plants will grow eight feet long.

WILL SCARLET

Semi-double flowers of scarlet are a delight on this landscape plant. It blooms repeatedly throughout the season, with colorful orange hips.

SHRUB

This class is a "catchall" for roses that don't fit into the other categories. Shrubs are of varied parentage but are generally large, hardy, and disease resistant.

GOLDEN WINGS

Large, single blooms of sulphur-yellow are graceful, slightly fragrant, and flower again and again. Stamens are prominent; attractive.

SEA FOAM

A sea of double, slightly fragrant, creamy-white flowers borne in clusters envelop this trailing plant all summer. The flexible, normally arching canes can climb a medium-size trellis, weep down an embankment, or form a handsome ground cover.

SPARRIESHOOP

Large, single, light pink flowers bloom off and on all season on an upright plant. It can grow 12 feet tall.

Sea Foam is versatile enough to fit into any landscape plan.

Belinda will easily produce masses of spectacular color, even in partial shade.

Hybrid Tea Roses

The classic beauty of the rose is defined in the hybrid teas. As the long pointed buds open, they reveal swirls of petals and elegant, high-centered blooms in every color but blue. There's hardly one that doesn't emit that fine and famous rose fragrance from flowers on plants two to five feet high. Alone or by the dozen, the hybrid tea is the perfect flower for a vase, perched proudly upon a long cutting stem. Pick one of the following and you won't be disappointed.

AMERICAN HERITAGE
Large and long double flowers of creamy yellow tickled with pink bloom on tall, upright plants. Slightly tender.

ANTIGUA
The blooms are double, golden apricot, and fragrant; the petals are wavy; the plant, tall. Like most varieties this color, it is tender.

APOLLO
Medium yellow, loose, fragrant flowers cover this tall plant. It's good for garden display, and the foliage is disease-resistant.

BEWITCHED
Large, silky pink flowers with a damask fragrance bloom profusely on a vigorous plant. This variety will commonly grow to 4 feet tall.

BIG BEN
Large, perfectly formed, heavily fragrant flowers are dark, velvety red and bloom freely on a tall bush.

BLUE MOON
Like all mauves, Blue Moon is very fragrant. The flowers of lilac blue cover an upright, medium-size plant.

CANDY STRIPE
This sport of Pink Peach has large, fully double, cupped-shaped, and fragrant blooms that are streaked in shades of pink and white on a plant of medium height. Use Candy Stripe with other roses or alone as a unique specimen plant.

CARLA
Soft pink petals with salmon undertones form a double, fragrant flower gracing a medium plant. Tender.

CENTURY TWO
Large, pale pink flowers are fragrant and shaded slightly darker on the outside of the petals; they're borne on a medium-height plant.

CHARLOTTE ARMSTRONG
A famous parent of many roses, this is a tall, bushy plant with full, loose, fragrant flowers of deep pink to light red.

CHICAGO PEACE
Identical to Peace except for the flower color, which varies in shades of yellow, bronze, and deep pink.

CHRISTIAN DIOR
All plants are adorned with double, glowing, cherry red blossoms that are slightly fragrant. Plants are compact and tall.

CHRYSLER IMPERIAL
A classic among reds, this very fragrant, large, perfectly formed rose blooms on a medium-size plant. At its best in warm weather. Hardier than other varieties.

COLOR MAGIC
Never the same twice, the petals of this rose change color from ivory to pink, coral, and rose. The blooms are large; the plant is medium size. Tender in cold climates.

COLUMBUS QUEEN
This well-branched, vigorous fragrant variety easily produces masses of 4- to 4½-inch pink, cupped flowers. Petals are slightly darker on the reverse side.

COMMAND PERFORMANCE
Reflexed petals give a star shape to this fragrant, orange-red rose that blooms on a very vigorous and tall plant.

CONFIDENCE
Large, sweetly fragrant blooms of pearly light pink are shaded in peach and yellow. Of medium height, it prefers warm climates. Stems are long and slender.

CRIMSON GLORY
Cupped, large flowers are deep, velvety red and extremely fragrant. The plant is low-growing and spreading.

DAINTY BESS
This single, 5-petalled flower is fragrant, soft rose pink, and set off by maroon stamens. Vigorous and free-blooming.

DIAMOND JUBILEE
Large, double, fragrant flowers are buff yellow to apricot on a plant of medium height. Growth is upright and compact; foliage, dark green and leathery. A good choice for mass planting or mixed rose border.

DOUBLE DELIGHT
A delight to look at and smell—with white petals edged in raspberry red to form a perfect flower on a low, spreading plant.

DUET
A rose of medium height that almost never stops producing fragrant, sparkling pink flowers with a deep pink reverse.

ECLIPSE
This rose first bloomed on the day of an eclipse in 1932 and is at its best in its golden yellow bud stage.

EIFFEL TOWER
The plant towers over others in the rose garden; the flowers are high-centered, very fragrant, and medium pink. The bushes are upright, vigorous, and very free-flowering.

ELECTRON
Thorny stems are topped with glowing pink, fragrant blooms, produced freely on a bushy, medium-size plant.

FIRST LOVE
Long, slender buds and flowers of pearly pink are attractive and fragrant on a tall plant or in a vase. A tender variety in cold areas.

FIRST PRIZE
Perfection in flower form is found on this fragrant rose with ivory pink centers, deeper pink outside.

FRAGRANT CLOUD
Clusters of orange-red flowers carry a heavy fragrance and bloom freely on a low- to medium-growing bush.

FRIENDSHIP
Friendship has sweet, fragrant, flesh-colored flowers.

GARDEN PARTY
This white, floriferous plant produces large, high-centered flowers.

GRANADA
Fragrant flowers are a luscious mix of red, gold, yellow, and pink over crinkled foliage. Slightly tender.

GRAND SLAM

Vigorous and bigger than average, this variety has superb form from bud through bloom. Excellent for cutting and can provide a source of long-stemmed flowers.

GYPSY
Buds almost black in color open into dark orange-red, fiery double flowers with a spicy fragrance. The plants grow tall.

HEIRLOOM
Semi-double, magenta flowers lighten to lilac as they age. Richly fragrant and decorative.

HELEN TRAUBEL
Tall plants produce apricot-pink, fragrant flowers often troubled by a weak neck.

IRISH GOLD

Fragrant, medium-yellow blooms are pointed and often tinged with pink. The plant grows low and tender.

ISABEL de ORTIZ
Well-formed flowers of deep pink with a silver reverse are large, double, and fragrant. Borne on long stems on a tall plant. Tender.

JADIS
Slender, very fragrant blooms of rose-pink top an upright, tall plant.

JOHN F. KENNEDY
Large, graceful, pointed buds appear on the tender plants all summer long, opening to reveal 3- or 4-inch dazzling white flowers. Foliage is dark green and disease-free. With good growing conditions the upright plants will grow to 4 feet tall.

Columbus Queen is a shapely, orchid-tinted pink with handsome foliage. Its long stems are almost thorn-free.

KING'S RANSOM

Almost perfect golden yellow, fragrant blooms sit atop long cutting stems. Tender in cold climates. Foliage is glossy green.

KORDES' PERFECTA

Creamy-white petals, tipped with crimson, on a fragrant, double flower grace this tall plant. The color darkens as the temperature climbs.

LADY X

High-centered blooms of pale pinkish lavender are slightly fragrant on this, the tallest and most vigorous of the mauve roses.

LEMON SPICE

The name says it all—lemon yellow blooms with a spicy fragrance. The plant is tall and spreading; the stems, weak and often thin.

MATTERHORN

Yellow, tinted buds open into high-centered, large, ivory-white flowers atop this very tall plant.

MEDALLION

Tall, robust plants produce equally large, light apricot blooms with a fruity fragrance and a crepe paper texture.

MICHELE MEILLAND

As feminine as its name, this creamy-pink, perfectly formed flower is shaded salmon in the center. It's a medium grower and a vigorous bloomer.

MIRANDY

This old-timer in rose gardens has an old-fashioned fragrance and double, deep red flowers on a compact, bushy plant. At its best where the weather is warm and humid.

MISS ALL-AMERICAN BEAUTY

So dark pink it's almost red, this large, cupped, double, very fragrant rose blooms on a plant of medium height.

MISTER LINCOLN

This tall, long-stemmed, high-centered fragrant beauty is one of the best of the dark reds.

MOJAVE

The colors of the desert shine red, apricot, and orange on a tall, slender flower and plant of the same shape.

NEUE REVUE

The plant's tall and so thorny you can hardly touch it; the flower is chalky white, edged in bright red. Double and fragrant.

OKLAHOMA

So dark red it's almost black, Oklahoma is tall and sturdy with velvety, very fragrant flowers.

OLDTIMER

Oldtimer produces masses of yellow-bronze flowers all summer long. Blooms are large, often reaching 7 inches in diameter.

OREGOLD

The blooms are large, loose, and deep gold that does not fade. Fragrant on a medium-size bush.

PAPA MEILLAND

Very fragrant, dark, velvety crimson blooms open slowly and adorn an erect, medium-growing plant.

PARADISE

Magnificent, perfectly shaped blooms of silvery mauve are shaded to pink at the center and highlighted by petals with red edges. The flowers are fragrant on tall, strong stems.

PASCALI

The bloom is small but perfectly formed, creamy white, and dependable, with a touch of fragrance on a tall plant.

PEACE

This timeless favorite is very full, light to golden yellow, and flushed with pink on the edges of a medium-size, spreading plant.

PEER GYNT

Tall and husky, this bush has large, full, golden yellow flowers with a touch of red on the edges of the petals as it ages. It's tender but bounces back quickly.

PERFUME DELIGHT

As the name says, the rose is richly fragrant with intense, old rose pink flowers of classic form on a medium-size plant. Plants are very disease resistant.

PHARAOH

Brilliant red, velvet-like flowers on long stems perfect for cutting. The plants are vigorous and tall.

PINK PEACE

The name is misleading, because this is not a pink duplicate of Peace but is tall and bushy with very fragrant flowers of deep, dusty pink.

PORTRAIT

The bush is tall and never without medium-size, fragrant blooms of blended pinks and ivory.

PRISTINE

Feminine purity best describes the delicate white with pink picotee, lightly fragrant flowers that bloom on a slightly tender plant of medium height. Use Pristine alone as a specimen plant, or mix with other hybrid teas.

Perfume Delight is all its name implies. A delightful, spicy fragrance escapes when the bright pink flowers unfold.

PROMISE
Pure, clear, dawn-pink flowers are large, high-centered, and lightly fragrant on a tall plant.

PROUD LAND
This brilliant red, flowering rose easily grows 6 feet tall. Blooms are fragrant and often measure 6 inches in diameter. Stems are long.

RED DEVIL

Large, very double blooms of bright, medium red have a silvery reverse and a pleasing fragrance on a plant of medium height.

RED LION
Thick, cherry-red petals form a perfect, high-centered flower on a medium tall bush.

RED MASTERPIECE
The flowers on this medium to tall rose are double, high centered, very fragrant, and deep red, marred only by petal edges sensitive to sunlight.

ROSE GAUJARD
Plant grows tall and very wide. Double, fragrant flowers of cherry red with a reverse of pale pink and silvery white. Here's one hybrid tea that likes a little shade.

ROYAL HIGHNESS
It's very tender but has perfectly formed, soft pale pink, very fragrant flowers that make it worth the effort to grow this tall plant.

RUBAIYAT
A hardy, vigorous bloomer, Rubaiyat produces large rose-red flowers all season. Foliage is dark green and attractive.

SEASHELL
The flowers are small but very numerous in luminous shades of shrimp pink, peach, and coral; they're strongly fragrant. The plant is of medium height and branches heavily. Slightly tender.

SILVER LINING
Very fragrant blooms of silvery pink have darker pink edges and a slightly cupped form. The tender plant is a medium grower.

SNOWFIRE
Bright scarlet petals are a blaze of color on a pure white reverse. The flowers are large, double, and open; the plants, compact and tender.

SOUTH SEAS
Large, frilled flowers open flat and fragrant in shades of soft salmon to coral pink on long stems and on a spreading plant.

SPELLBINDER
As ivory buds unfurl, the roses begin to take on a pink blush that grows deeper and deeper, until the large, double flowers end up a rose-red. A tender plant of medium height.

STERLING SILVER
The original lavender rose, Sterling Silver produces medium-size, slightly fragrant flowers. Foliage is dark, glossy, and attractive. Stems are long.

SUMMER SUNSHINE
The brightest of the yellow roses is large, full, and fragrant and on a medium to tall plant. Tender in cold climates. The color doesn't fade.

SUNSET JUBILEE
Very large, high-centered blooms of coppery pink with light yellow tints become more brilliant as the weather warms up. The medium-tall plant is almost never out of bloom.

SUSAN MASSU
Long thorny stems are clothed with fragrant, high-centered blooms of light yellow, tipped with a blush of light pink.

SUTTER'S GOLD
Orange and rust-red buds open into very fragrant, large, golden orange flowers with scarlet veining and petal edges. In cool weather, the tall plant produces blooms of more vibrant color.

SWARTHMORE
Tall, somewhat tender plants have slightly fragrant, high-centered flowers of cherry pink to dusty rose, with petals edged in gray. Plants are vigorous, bushy, and free-flowering.

TIFFANY
Long buds open to reveal delicate pink flowers with a yellow base. Famous for their heavy fragrance and long-cutting stems. Foliage is dark green and attractive.

TORO
Many say this is the same rose as Uncle Joe. Both have enormous buds that unfurl slowly into large, strongly perfumed, dark red flowers on long, strong stems.

TROPICANA
The first of the fluorescent coral-orange roses is still one of the most popular, with perfectly formed, fruity-scented flowers on a tall, spreading plant.

WHITE KNIGHT
Large, pure white, high-centered flowers appear on long stems all season long. Plants are vigorous and upright with attractive light green foliage.

WHITE MASTERPIECE
Compact, spreading plants produce very large, ruffled pure white double flowers on a very thick penduncle. Slightly tender in cold climate areas. Very disease resistant.

WINI EDMUNDS
High, reflexed flowers are strawberry colored, with a straw yellow reverse and moderately fragrant on a tall plant. Tender.

YANKEE DOODLE
Large, globular flowers of light yellow are flushed with apricot and salmon, fragrant, and produced on a upright, bushy plant. Tender in cold climates. Plants are vigorous and hardy with attractive olive-green foliage. A good specimen plant in almost any location.

A sure favorite in any garden, Double Delight is hardy, long-stemmed, and fragrant, with disease-resistant foliage.

Grandifloras

A compromise in the rose garden is the grandiflora, which exhibits the best traits of its parents, the hybrid tea and the floribunda. From the hybrid tea it inherits flower form and long cutting stems; from the floribunda it receives hardiness, continuous flowering, and clusters of blooms generally at the same stage of development. The unique thing about most members of this class is that they grow taller than either parent. You can plant the grandiflora at the back of the border, or use it as a screen.

AQUARIUS
Long, tight buds open into perfectly formed flowers that are blended in pinks and mildly fragrant. The blooms are produced one per stem or in clusters on a tall, slender plant.

ARIZONA
Large, double flowers are the colors of an Arizona sunset—orange, gold, copper, and pink—very fragrant and blooming on a medium-size, upright, and slightly tender plant.

CAMELOT
Double, cup-shaped, decorative blooms are coral-pink and bloom in clusters on a vigorous bush.

CARROUSEL
Because this plant is very tall, place it in the background. The vivid flowers are semi-double, dark red, and lightly scented in small clusters.

COMANCHE
Bold, brick-red to orange blooms are large, double, and well formed. The flowers appear singly and in clusters, are quick to repeat, and have a slight fragrance.

JOHN S. ARMSTRONG
Slightly fragrant, double, cupped flowers are vivid dark red and bloom freely on a tall plant.

MONTEZUMA
Coral-orange and terra-cotta in color, double, high-centered blooms have a slight scent. The plants are tall and do best in moist climates.

MOUNT SHASTA
Seemingly as high as a mountain, this rose has blooms as beautiful in bud as they are when the large, fragrant white flowers are open. It is not at its best in midsummer heat.

OLÉ
The double, orange-red blooms are ruffled and frilled and look like a camellia. The fragrant flowers appear profusely above dark green, holly-like foliage.

PINK PARFAIT
Pastel pink, double blooms, teamed up with abundant foliage, are together so thick you can barely see the canes of this medium-size plant.

PROMINENT
It's short for a grandiflora, but the bright orange-red, star-shaped flowers more than make up for it.

QUEEN ELIZABETH
The symbol of perfection among grandifloras is this tall rose with radiant carmine to dawn pink, fragrant blooms in clusters.

SCARLET KNIGHT
Large, slightly fragrant, velvety crimson to scarlet, high-centered flowers bloom heavily on a medium size, bushy plant.

SONIA
The flowers are satiny, small, and on the coral side of pink; the plants are low-growing and tender in cold climates.

Floribundas

The floribunda, or landscape rose, is a cross between the flower form of the hybrid tea and the abundant blooms of the polyantha. Sprays that flower nearly all the time contain every stage of bloom, from tight buds to fully open flowers, on long cutting stems. Floribundas are hardier, lower-growing, and bushier than most hybrid teas, making them a perfect choice for hedges, massing, or borders. On top of all this, the mounded plants show every rose color available and are relatively free of disease.

ACCENT
Sprays of medium, decorative flowers bloom profusely on a low-growing, compact plant, perfect for low hedges and edgings.

ANABELL
Fragrant, rich orange-salmon, showy flowers bloom all summer in large sprays on a low to medium plant. This variety is slightly tender.

ANGEL FACE
Deep lavender, wavy flowers are fragrant and semi-double, opening quickly to show off golden stamens on a low, mounding plant.

APACHE TEARS
Scarlet edges tint the classically formed white flowers that appear one per stem or in clusters on short, upright plants. This variety is slightly tender.

APRICOT NECTAR
Large sprays of double, cupped, creamy apricot flowers are touched with pink and gold and have a very fruity fragrance. The plants are medium-tall, bushy, vigorous, and will not fade out in bright sun.

BAHIA
Double, cupped, orange-red flowers have a golden yellow reverse and a spicy fragrance. Good for massing, the plants are upright and bushy. Plants bloom in large attractive clusters and can be grown as a showy hedge, barrier plantings, or property dividers.

BETTY PRIOR
Growing tall and wide, the plants produce sprays of single, carmine pink, fragrant flowers.

BON BON
Flowers of hybrid tea form are rose-pink with a silvery reverse, blooming in trusses on low-growing plants. Blooms are slightly fragrant and appear all summer long, until the first frost.

CATHEDRAL

Wavy, open flowers on a medium-size bush are vibrant orange with a touch of yellow. They're sweetly fragrant.

CHARISMA
Brilliant orange and gold tones jump from the sprays of flowers that bloom continuously on very low-growing plants. They're excellent for massing or bedding. Flowers are long-lasting and weather resistant.

CIRCUS

Fragrant double flowers are yellow with red edges, becoming more and more red as the blooms age. The plant is low-growing and spreading.

CITY OF BELFAST

Small, double, cupped blooms of metallic orange-red flower in large trusses on a low-growing plant. Ideal for a hedge or foreground.

ELSE POULSEN

Semi-double, slightly fragrant flowers are bright rose-pink, blooming in sprays on a medium-size, bushy plant.

EUROPEANA

Blooms are dark crimson, large, double, and decorative in very large and heavy trusses. New red foliage adorns low, spreading plants.

EVENING STAR

These flowers look like a cross between the bloom form of the hybrid tea and the spray of the floribunda. Flowers of pure white glisten on tender plants of medium height.

FABERGE

Neat, compact plants are clothed in small, warm peach-pink flowers in tight sprays. This one will even stand partial shade.

FASHION

Lively coral and peachy-pink flowers are double and fragrant, opening flat in large sprays on a low, bushy plant that will grow 3 feet tall. Blooms are long-lasting, storm-resistant, and about 3½ inches in diameter.

FIRE KING

Tall, vigorous bushes are clustered with fiery orange-red to scarlet flowers that are free-blooming and musk scented.

FIRST EDITION

Large, double, bright coral blooms are held on good-sized but short-stemmed trusses. The plants are of medium height and spreading.

GENE BOERNER

The medium pink flowers are petite replicas of a perfect hybrid tea, with a slight luminescence and a sweet fragrance. Plants are upright of medium height, with blooms in small inflorescences.

GINGER

Tropicana coral-orange-colored blooms are large, cupped, fragrant, and openly decorative on a low, compact, bushy plant.

ICEBERG

About the tallest of the floribundas, it has pure white, open, double, very fragrant flowers in loose, carefree sprays, set off by light green foliage.

A good choice for edging a walk, driveway, or evergreen planting.

IVORY FASHION

Long buds open slowly into flat, semi-double, fragrant flowers of ivory white on a short to middle-size plant.

LITTLE DARLING

The flowers are little and darling, a blend of yellow and soft pink, with a spicy fragrance. The plants, on the other hand, are large and spreading, bearing flower sprays on arching stems.

MATADOR

Small, startling blooms are a blend of orange and gold, slightly ruffled on a compact, dense plant.

ORANGEADE

Bright, pure orange, semi-double flowers bloom in large sprays on husky and slightly spreading plants.

PICNIC

Here's a vigorous, free-blooming plant of medium height, with flowers of coral that have a yellow base and a tinge of pink.

REDGOLD

Medium, double, slightly fragrant flowers are, as the name implies, gold, edged in red. Plants are neat, low- to medium-growing, and tender. An effective landscaping plant, even though the flowers are slightly smaller than other floribundas. In some locations, Redgold may occasionally look a bit rangy. Blooms appear singly, as well as in large clusters, and turn darker with age.

A good choice for most any landscaping situation, Redgold produces masses of long-lasting, showy flowers.

ROSE PARADE

Masses of shrimp pink, large, open, cupped flowers are fragrant and bloom in small sprays on a round and compact, medium-size bush. The double flowers will bloom up to 4 inches across. Rose Parade is very hardy, disease-resistant, and well shaped. Plants will bloom continuously.

SARABANDE

Semi-double, orange-red flowers open flat to show off bright yellow stamens on a low-growing, sprawling plant. Sarabande blooms continuously all season long, with flowers that measure up to 4 inches across. A good choice for larger gardens.

SARATOGA

Low-spreading plants with many branches are smothered in gardenia-like, very fragrant white flowers. Plants will grow 3 feet tall and are hardy in most areas.

SEA PEARL

Buds of pastel pink open into flowers of pearly pink, diffused with peach and yellow. The tall plants generally produce one bloom per stem. Foliage is dark green and attractive; plants upright, bushy, and hardy. Blossoms open to 4½ inches.

SPANISH SUN

Deep golden yellow blooms are large, hybrid tea-shaped, extremely scented, and excellent as cut flowers or as a garden display on a bushy

plant. Blooms measure 2½ to 3 inches across and will often appear on stems up to 10 inches long. Foliage is dark green and shiny.

SPARTAN

Small sprays of orange- to coral-colored, high-centered, very fragrant blooms appear on vigorous plants of medium height. Many blooms are borne singly on slender graceful stems.

SUNSPRITE

Deep, bright, sunny yellow flowers are large, fragrant, and early-blooming on a tidy, very disease-resistant plant. Blooms will measure 3 inches across.

TAMANGO

Disease-resistant, tall- and wide-growing plants are covered with carefree, massive sprays of velvety crimson flowers.

VOGUE

Slender buds open to fragrant, cherry-coral flowers.

WOBURN ABBEY

Bushy, tall-growing plants produce large sprays of orange, fragrant, medium-size flowers that are shaded with red and gold.

POLYANTHA

If you're looking for a rose that is low-growing, compact, blooms continually, and is very hardy, the polyantha is for you. The flowers are small and of informal shape, like pompons, and massed over the plant in very large clusters. Try polyanthas for bedding, low hedges, and foregrounds. Although many polyanthas have been replaced in the rose garden by their larger-growing and showier relatives, the floribundas, several are still worth growing. Blossoms rarely get over 2 inches across, but when in flower, this group of roses is famous for colorful display.

CECILE BRUNNER

This is the original "Sweetheart" rose, with small, double, perfectly formed, light pink-on-yellow flowers of moderate fragrance.

CHINA DOLL

Dense clusters of bright pink, tiny flowers bloom continually and almost hide the low-growing bush that's perfect for a border. Most specimens will grow 18 inches tall. Foliage is leathery and attractive.

MARGO KOSTER

Double, salmon flowers are globular and shaped like tiny ranunculus. The low-growing bushes make good potted plants or edgings. Flowers are slightly fragrant, borne in small clusters. A good choice for greenhouse culture.

THE FAIRY

Use this bushy plant of medium height as a hedge or in the shrub border for everblooming, cone-shaped clusters of delicate, light pink flowers. It grows 2 to 3 feet tall and quickly forms a hardy, compact bush. It's very resistant to insects and disease and will even flower abundantly in partial shade. The Fairy is a good variety for low-maintenance gardens.

One rose no garden should be without is Spartan. It's always spectacular, with a truly delightful fragrance.

Tree Roses

Tree roses, otherwise known as standards, are the crowning glory of the rose garden. If you want to view your favorite blooms at eye level, plant them in the form of tree roses. They will accent a bed, dress up an entrance, or decorate a patio. Formal gardens are perfect sites for tree roses, as is any spot needing a certain air of distinction. You will have to see the beauty of a tree of roses for yourself to appreciate what it can do as a highlight in your garden.

Tree roses are the man-made plants of the rose garden. Onto a root understock is grafted a stem of *Rosa multiflora, R. rugosa,* De la Grifferaie, or a similar strong grower. Onto the stem is budded any bush rose there is—hybrid tea, floribunda, grandiflora, polyantha, miniature, climber. The process is a long one, which makes tree roses more expensive than other roses, but their well-proportioned, full, and wide heads of color make them worth the price.

Tree roses vary in height. Most have trunks three feet tall, but there are others only two feet tall that are perfect for patios, garden apartments, and small terraces. Minis are usually grafted onto an 18-inch trunk, forming an 18-inch ball of color atop it. And occasionally you will see a six-foot tree rose with the canes of a climber tumbling down from the top.

Flowers of tree roses are the same as the flowers of the original bush roses—and better. The color is the same, the blooms larger, of better form, and more freely produced.

Roses available as standards vary from year to year. When choosing yours, pick one of the spreading, rather than upright, varieties for a full, round head three to four feet across. One of the floribundas would be most colorful, and a tree rose of The Fairy or of Sea Foam is spectacular as a light and graceful cloud of blooms.

When planting tree roses, place a stake next to the trunk, and secure the trunk to it in three places with soft ties that will not damage the bark. The stake should extend into the head; it will be hidden by the flowers. Supports can be of metal or decay-resistant wood. Because the bark of the tree is very sensitive to the sun, place the stake on the sunny side, or wrap the trunk in burlap.

When planting a tree rose, remember it is a specimen of beauty, so choose its home carefully. Because the eye will be drawn to it, the background must be complementary and at least as attractive. A light-colored rose against a dark background will make the tree stand out even more. After you have the tree rose in place, especially if warm spring weather is fast approaching, wrap the canes in moist sphagnum moss, or pop a plastic bag over the tree's head. This will prevent the canes from drying out and will help them to sprout more quickly. Just be sure to remove either as soon as the buds break into leaf.

Consider planting tree roses in decorative containers. Not only will you be able to move your specimens around, it will also be easier to protect them in winter. Simply bring the containers indoors into a frost-free area. High in the sky as they are and therefore even more exposed to the rigors of winter, tree roses are the most sensitive to cold and wind and must be heavily protected in all but the mildest of climates.

Climbing Roses

Climbing roses are not climbers in the true sense of the word; they do not send out tendrils and need to be tied to their supports (with a few exceptions). Climbers are really long caned, pliable roses that will usually produce many more flowers if trained horizontally. The class includes climbers that produce loose clusters of large flowers on fairly hardy plants and climbing sports of hybrid teas, grandifloras, floribundas, and polyanthas. The climbing sports have flowers identical to their parents' (sometimes of better quality), but the bushes are not so hardy.

Some climbers are referred to as pillar roses, because they grow smaller, more upright, and with stiffer canes.

ALOHA
Long-stemmed clusters of large, cup-shaped, fragrant, medium rose-pink flowers (with a deeper reverse) bloom recurrently on a climber that grows best on a pillar. A climbing hybrid tea, not a sport of a bush rose.

AMERICA
Slow to climb, easy to train, this large-flowered climber is a bright coral pink, opening from salmon buds. The flowers are large, pointed, spice scented, and seem to glow all summer. The plant is easy to keep just where you want it.

BLAZE
Most nurseries sell the improved strain that blooms heavily in June and fairly regularly all summer. Flowers are medium, semi-double, bright scarlet, cupped, and slightly fragrant. They form in large clusters on an easy grower. Large-flowered climber.

CHEVY CHASE
Chevy Chase is a fine addition to fence or garden wall. This rambler rose carries masses of dark red bloom at the end of each cane. Plants are very vigorous but bloom heavily only once a season. With good growing conditions, mature specimens will grow 15 feet tall.

CORAL DAWN
Large, coral to rose-pink double, the cupped flowers have satiny petals and a pleasing fragrance.

DON JUAN
Slightly stiff stems make this large-flowered climber a good pillar rose. Blooms are dark velvety red, very fragrant, and perfectly formed on long-cutting stems. Tips freeze in cold winters but snap back fast.

DR. J. H. NICOLAS
Large, globular flowers of medium rose-pink are borne in small sprays that give the plant an airy look. The large double blooms are fragrant, and the plant does well on a pillar or trellis. Large-flowered climber.

GOLDEN SHOWERS
Stems of this large-flowered climber are so strong and stiff that it can stand unsupported as a large shrub. Try it on a trellis, too, but it's a little too upright for a fence. Repeating, semi-double flowers are loose, fragrant, and daffodil yellow.

HANDEL
Clusters of wavy, frilled, double flowers are ivory edged in deep rose-pink to red. The strong plant grows quickly and repeats fairly well all summer. Large-flowered climber.

HIGH NOON
Bright, sunny yellow flowers are tinted with red in a double, loose, cupped form. Blooms bear a spicy fragrance and recur on a large and rampant climbing hybrid tea. Individual canes will grow 8 feet or more in length. Foliage is glossy, dark green, and, with good care, is attractive all season long.

JOSEPH'S COAT

Multi-colored, like the Biblical garb for which it was named, this large-flowered climber has buds of orange and red opening into yellow blooms that pass through shades of orange and scarlet as they age. The small fluffy flowers are showy all season on a vigorous pillar rose. Tender.

NEW DAWN

This sport of Dr. W. Van Fleet is identical to it in all respects, except that it blooms repeatedly. Flowers are of the palest pink, double but opening fast on a very large and vigorous plant.

PAUL'S SCARLET CLIMBER

This large-flowered climber is similar to Blaze, its offspring, except that it rarely repeats bloom. The plants are very vigorous, with bright scarlet, weather-resistant flowers borne in large clusters. Foliage is dark green, glossy, attractive, and disease resistant. Plants can grow 16 to 20 feet tall.

PINATA

Similar to Joseph's Coat, but with large flowers, this large-flowered climber has sunshine-yellow blooms, diffused with orange and red. The plant repeats consistently and is so neat and strong it can stand alone as a shrub.

RED FOUNTAIN

Arching canes are filled with sprays of velvety, dark red, ruffled, and cupped double blooms. The fragrance is reminiscent of an old-fashioned rose. Plants are strong and may be trained against supports or left without staking. Large-flowered climber.

RHONDA

Clusters of large, double, salmon-pink flowers bloom heavily on a strong, large-flowered climber.

ROYAL GOLD

Deep yellow, non-fading flowers are moderately fragrant, blooming heavily in June and showing some repeat during the summer. The large-flowered climber is stiff and compact. Tender.

ROYAL SUNSET

Hybrid tea-shaped flowers are large, double, and a deep, rich apricot, fading to light peach in summer heat. The large-flowered climber has a fruity fragrance. Tender.

TALISMAN

Medium-size, yellow-bronze flowers appear on long, slender stems. Blooms open flat, with a strong, pleasant fragrance. The foliage is light green, glossy, and attractive all season. Talisman is easily trained and makes a good choice for arbor or trellis. A vigorous grower in most areas.

TEMPO

Very double, high-centered, deep red flowers bloom in clusters on a tidy, large-flowered climber. An early bloomer, this variety will often be the first climber in the garden to show bloom. Flowers vary between 3 and 4 inches in diameter and are extra showy. Blooms are long lasting and weather resistant. Tempo is a vigorous grower and very disease resistant.

WHITE DAWN

Gardenia-like, snow-white, semi-double flowers are everblooming, fragrant, and clustered on this, the first and still the best white, large-flowered climber. It's hardy, vigorous, and will quickly spread over a large area. Foliage is glossy and attractive.

In addition to these climbers, many popular bush roses have sported to produce climbers. These include Charlotte Armstrong, Chrysler Imperial, Crimson Glory, First Prize, Peace, Queen Elizabeth, Sutter's Gold, and Tropicana.

RAMBLERS

Decades ago, the climbing roses of the garden were the ramblers, descendants of *Rosa wichuraiana* and *R. multiflora.* They are huge and rampant growers, with small flowers appearing in one gorgeous flush of spring bloom. Many ramblers produce supple canes up to 30 feet long that must be pruned back after each bloom period to keep the plants in good condition. Ramblers are also very hardy, but because of their vast size, high maintenance, and limited bloom, they have all but disappeared from the rose marketplace. Replacing them are the large-flowered climbers and climbing hybrid teas of today, which bloom freely, continually, and easily from early spring, right up until frost. Some ramblers are still popular, however, in far northern latitudes.

Enjoy the beauty of Chevy Chase added to fence or garden wall. It carries red flowers at the end of each cane.

Miniature Roses

There is something very precious about a tiny reproduction —whether it be a baby, a dollhouse, or a rose. It won't take long for the charm and attraction of miniature roses to get to you. On a mini, everything is small—the flowers, the leaves, the plant. Plant sizes range from 3 to 4 inches for a micro-mini to 18 inches for a tall grower, with all heights in between. For growing minis in an indoor garden, best results are achieved with one of the lower growing and more compact plants.

BABY BETSY MCCALL
Beautifully formed, dainty, light pink buds and flowers, with just a hint of cream at the base of the petals, grace a mid-size plant.

BABY DARLING
Tulip-shaped buds and free-flowering apricot blooms top this easy-to-grow plant of medium height. There is also a climbing form.

BABY MASQUERADE
Blooms on this mini change from yellow to orange and red as the flowers open and mature. The plant grows tall; there is also a climbing form.

BEAUTY SECRET
This one is vigorous, upright, and tall, with long, pointed buds and medium-red, large, fragrant blooms.

BO-PEEP
This is a micro-mini with double soft pink flowers, always in bloom on a neat and compact plant, at times looking like an old-fashioned rose. Foliage is small, glossy, and very attractive.

CHIPPER
This tall, yet compact and bushy, mini is a blooming fool, with large, coral-pink flowers of excellent form and substance.

CINDERELLA
Dainty white flowers with a hint of pale dawn-pink sit atop this neat and compact micro-mini. There's also a climbing form. It's a good choice for both indoor and outdoor culture,

producing its fragrant flowers all year long if the plants are kept under grow-lights.

CUDDLES
Fully double, high-centered, reflexed, coral-pink blooms stand on a tall, vigorous plant. The foliage is small, glossy, and attractive.

DWARFKING
Dark red, well-shaped buds open flat into double flowers on a strong and bushy plant. Mature plants will grow 10 inches tall and bloom all season.

EASTER MORNING
Very double, fragrant, ivory-white flowers bloom abundantly on a bushy plant. Easter Morning will easily grow 16 inches tall.

FAIRY ROSE

This variety rarely gets over 1 foot tall but still manages to produce a profusion of attractive, rose-red, double flowers. Foliage is glossy and delicate.

GLORIGLO
Magnificent, glowing, fluorescent-orange, high-centered blooms have a white reverse and flower on an unusual and tall bush.

GOLD COIN
Blooms are yellow and open quickly to an attractive, flat, decorative form. The plant is a neat grower of medium height.

GREEN ICE
Apricot buds open into double white flowers that turn light green with age. It blooms in heavy clusters, which make it excellent for hanging baskets.

HULA GIRL
A fresh orange fragrance and a bright, orange-yellow double bloom remind one of a South Pacific sunset. Small, firm foliage covers a bushy, medium plant.

JANNA
Flowers are white with pinkish-red edges; the plant is tall and vigorous.

JEANIE WILLIAMS
Small red and yellow bicolor blooms make this an excellent plant of medium height.

JEANNE LAJOIE
Medium-pink, double flowers have hybrid tea form and bloom repeatedly on this climbing miniature that also doubles well in a hanging basket or window box.

JUDY FISCHER

Profuse flowers have perfect exhibition form and are a medium rose-pink. The plant is tall and strong.

KATHY
Fragrant blooms are rich red with white at the base of the petals on a plant of medium height.

KATHY ROBINSON
Pink with buff reverse flowers top this mini whose blooms repeat well on a tall, bushy plant.

LAVENDER LACE
Very double, fragrant, large flowers of lilac decorate a plant of medium height.

LITTLEST ANGEL
This micro-mini has fragrant, medium-yellow flowers blooming continually on a compact bush.

MAGIC CARROUSEL
One of the best, the plant is tall, the flowers double-white with red edges, the petals pointed and lacy.

MARY ADAIR
Soft, apricot flowers have excellent form and substance and bloom on a plant of medium height.

MARY MARSHALL
A perfect bud and high-centered exhibition flower of coral-orange with a yellow base make this mini a garden favorite.

OVER THE RAINBOW
This mini is tall, blooms profusely, and has striking, high-centered blooms of a unique blend of red and gold.

PIXIE ROSE
Small, very double, delicate flowers of deep rose-pink bloom freely on a dwarf, compact plant.

RED CASCADE
Hundreds of dark red flowers cover this spreading miniature. At home in a hanging basket or covering the ground.

ROSMARIN
A double micro-mini in a blend of pinks is a tiny replica of the perfect hybrid tea.

SCARLET GEM
Pointed petals of clear orange-red top this tall, upright plant. The flower is cupped and very double.

SEABREEZE
Cone-shaped clusters of medium-pink flowers have a hint of yellow at the base and a light, airy appearance.

SHERI ANNE
Good substance and form characterize the orange-red blooms that have a yellow base and flower on a tall plant.

SIMPLEX
Delightful and charming, this medium-size mini has only five petals of white, set off by bright yellow stamens.

STARINA
The favorite of them all has glowing, orange-red, fragrant flowers of classic form.

TOP SECRET
Deep red and fragrant flowers are almost identical to Beauty Secret (of which it is a sport) but with a few more petals.

TOY CLOWN
This high-centered and fragrant mini has white blooms with red edges, much like Magic Carrousel but with fewer petals and not as tall. Foliage is glossy and attractive.

The pale pink, Lavender Lace, resembles its floribunda cousins in shape of bloom and bushiness of foliage.

Basics of Rose Care

When do you plant roses? Bare-root roses are planted at times when they are dormant and the ground is not frozen. In warm areas, this is in late winter. Where winter temperatures do not go below 0° Fahrenheit, planting may be done in early spring or late fall. In areas of extreme cold, roses should be planted in spring only. Where possible, fall planting is preferred, because bushes are freshly dug and the roots will grow for much of the winter, leading to strong top growth in spring.

Bare-root roses, usually bought from mail order nurseries, should be planted as soon as possible after they arrive. If they have to be stored for several days before planting, put them in a cool place, and keep the roots moist by wetting them down and wrapping them in damp newspaper or plastic. If several weeks will pass before they can be planted, heel the roses in by burying the entire plant, canes and roots, in a trench in a cool, shaded spot.

Before planting, soak bare-root roses in a bucket of water or mud for six to 24 hours. This will restore moisture to the canes lost during shipping.

Before you place roses in the ground, think ahead. Place them where they can stay put and will not have to be moved in two or three years. Set your roses where they will receive at least six hours of full sun a day, preferably in the morning. Where summer heat becomes intense, help them gain relief from high temperatures and glare by placing them in a spot that gets light afternoon shade. Miniatures will tolerate a little more shade than their larger cousins and are very happy in the dappled shade of an ornamental tree.

Don't plant roses where their roots will compete with roots from other trees and shrubs. If this is impossible, install underground barriers made from impenetrable and durable material, such as an asbestos shingle or aluminum siding. Place it so the competing roots will stay away from the roses, yet give the rose roots room to grow.

If at all possible, keep roses out of drying winds by using a fence, living hedge, or other break. High winds will also damage or destroy open flowers. And as pretty as a ground cover may look, don't put it in a spot near the roses where it might steal food and water.

HOW TO PLANT A ROSE

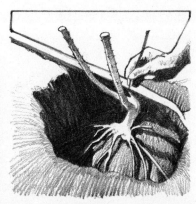

Locate the bud union, which is the point where the rose was grafted to the understock. It is easy to recognize as a knob on top of the root shank at the base of the canes. It should be placed just above ground level after planting because sun helps in the formation of basal breaks. In areas with cold winters, it will need to be protected from freezing.

After the planting hole is dug, place a mound of improved soil in the bottom of it. Set the plant on top of the cone of soil, spreading out the roots evenly on all sides. Lay a broom or shovel handle across the rim of the hole, using it to position the bud union correctly. Place it slightly above ground level; it will sink. Be sure to keep the roots moist as you work.

A rose is no better than the soil it is planted in, so take a few minutes to improve the good earth. Drainage is of utmost importance; roses do not like wet feet. Dig a hole large enough to hold a gallon of water. Fill it. If it drains in an hour, don't worry. If it doesn't, improve the drainage by adding perlite, vermiculite, or coarse sand, setting drainage tiles or terracing.

Soil should be light and rich to guarantee good growth, so improve it by adding organic matter such as peat moss, leaf mold, compost, or well-rotted manure. Organic enrichment should be a quarter of the total soil volume. Heavy clay soils should be loosened with gypsum.

The pH is also important. For good roses, it should be between 6.0 and 6.5, a slightly acid reading. To get the soil to this level, use lime if your soil is more acidic and sulfur if it is on the alkaline side. Have a soil test done to be sure where you stand.

Good root growth is a sure thing if superphosphate is incorporated into the soil at planting time, but use no other fertilizer when planting. Prepare the soil deeply, to a depth of 24 inches, and you are ready to pick up your shovel.

Dig a hole about 18 inches deep and around, and plant the rose as illustrated below. Don't be afraid to prune away any broken roots or roots that are too long to fit into the planting hole without crowding.

In most climates, 24 inches between hybrid teas, grandifloras, or floribundas will be just right. Where winters are very mild and the roses have little dormancy, if any, plants may be spaced farther apart as they grow larger. For dense edging and hedges, space a little tighter. Shrub and old garden roses are spaced according to their size, about four to six feet apart in most cases. Climbers to be trained horizontally along a fence should be given a distance of eight to ten feet between plants. Miniatures are laid out depending on their height. Microminis can be as close as four inches; taller varieties should have 12 to 18 inches between plants.

If leaves are falling when you are planting your roses, add a border of crocus at the edge of the bed and clumps of daffodils between the plants. They will bring early color, and by the time they fade, the roses are almost ready to bloom.

The advantage of buying roses in containers is that the planting season

is extended throughout the summer, allowing you to fill in bits of color whenever or wherever it is needed.

Dig a hole larger and deeper than the container, and prepare the soil the same way as for bare-root roses. Place soil back in the hole so the bud union will be on the correct level after planting. Carefully remove the container, peel it away, or slit it with a knife, disturbing the root ball as little as possible. Holding the rose in place, firm soil around the roots by hand or with the help of a spade. Water well, stand back, and watch your rose grow.

Planting a rose into a decorative container is the same as planting it into the ground. Be sure the container has drainage holes, and for best results, use a soil-less potting medium. Commercial potting medium will provide all the nutrients your roses need and will be light enough to make all your containers extra portable.

After the rose is in place, remove the name tag if it is attached with wire. The wire might damage the cane. Even if it doesn't, the cane will one day be pruned away, and the tag may go with it. Use a plant label, and keep a record of what you plant.

Holding the rose straight and at the right level, back-fill the planting hole about two-thirds full. Gently tamp down the soil around the roots by hand or by stepping on it lightly. Fill the hole with water and allow it to drain, which will eliminate air pockets. After all the water is gone, fill the hole to the top with the improved soil mixture.

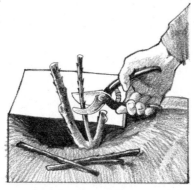

Prune the new roses back by a third, removing any dried or broken wood at the same time. The first few weeks of the rose's life are the most important, and it should never be allowed to dry out from sun or wind. Mound soil over the rose's canes approximately two-thirds of the way up the plant, and leave it in place until new growth is one to two inches long.

After the new growth is well developed, wash the soil mound away with a gentle stream of water from the garden hose. Be careful not to accidentally damage any new shoots that may be developing under the soil protection. Check all the plants one more time while waiting for bloom, and prune back any canes that may not have grown.

Pruning

It is sometimes difficult to take pruning shears in hand and cut away live wood from a rose bush. If you don't however, it will soon become tall and rangy and produce few good flowers. Pruning is needed to control the size and shape of a plant and keep it healthy, vigorous, and covered in bloom.

Pruning time comes when the buds begin to swell—but before they show signs of becoming a leaf. Depending on where you live, this will vary between midwinter and mid-spring. If forsythia grows in the neighborhood, prune your roses when yellow blooms show.

The correct tools of the trade are most important. A curved edged pruning shears, as large as your hand can comfortably hold, should be used, rather than the straight-edged, anvil variety that can crush the stems as it cuts. The only time anvil shears can be used, without damage, is in the removal of dead wood. Also, have on hand a long-handled lopping shear to cut out thick branches or tackle old garden and shrub roses and climbers. A pruning saw is a great aid in cutting out thick canes.

Make sure your pruning shears are sharp! If they become dull, sharpen the blade yourself, have it professionally sharpened, or buy a replacement blade. Jagged cuts from dull shears do not heal quickly and are prone to insects and disease.

Prune hybrid teas, floribundas, and grandifloras as illustrated below. In climates where winters are severe, the pruning height may be determined for you, depending on how much winterkill the plant experienced. If you can choose your heights, prune hybrid teas and floribundas to a height of 12 to 18 inches and grandifloras about six inches higher. Another good way to measure is to cut off a third to a half of the plant. There is no advantage to pruning a plant very low (six inches); it will not produce larger blooms. The higher a plant is pruned, the earlier it will bloom, but don't let this lead you to believe it should not be pruned—it must be, to keep it well groomed.

To control the spread of disease from one plant to another, swish your pruning shears in a half-and-half solution of household bleach and water each time you make a cut.

HOW TO PRUNE A ROSE

   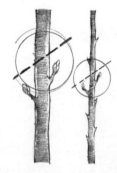

The first step in pruning rose bushes is to remove the winter protection, so you can see what you are dealing with. Cut away all dead and diseased wood first, pruning all dead canes flush with the bud union. Any branches that are broken, wounded, or have cankers should be pruned below the injury to the point where the pith is white and completely healthy.

Next, cut out weak or spindly branches, which generally will be smaller in diameter than your little finger. Canes that are growing into the center of the plant are removed next, along with those that crisscross each other. Keep the middle of the plant open to let in sunshine and allow air to circulate freely through the plant to discourage diseases.

By this time, you should be left with several good, strong canes. Select three or four of the newest and strongest canes to remain on the plant, removing all of the others flush with the bud union. Never leave short stumps on the bush, because insects and disease then have an entryway. For the same reason, do not leave short spurs higher on the canes.

Make all pruning cuts at a 45-degree angle, about ¼ inch above a bud and sloping downward from it, so water will run off freely. If too much cane is left above the bud, it will die back; if the cut is made too close, the bud may not survive. Wherever possible, prune to an outward facing bud, to keep the plant open and nicely shaped and to avoid tangled centers.

Blackspot spores spend the winter in the canes of a rose bush. If the disease was a problem last season, this is the one time you should prune your bushes lower than usual. You will cut away and discard many of your problems. Never leave cuttings lying between the roses. They, too, may carry disease.

Pruning cuts that are ½ inch or more in diameter may be sealed with a pruning compound, orange shellac, or grafting wax if boring insects are a problem in the area. Otherwise, sealing should not be necessary. White glue, which is often recommended as a sealant, is water soluble and will wash away in the first rain.

Floribundas used for hedges and masses of color may be pruned higher, with more canes remaining. Hybrid perpetuals should be taller than hybrid teas, and, because they bloom heaviest on last year's wood, should have only the oldest canes removed. Shrub and old garden roses are pruned primarily to remove old, weak, or dead wood or to correct misshapen growth. Leave them as large and natural as space permits.

Miniatures should be pruned according to how you are going to use them. If you like them petite, they may be pruned as low as three to four inches. If used as hedges and edgings, they may be left as tall as six to eight inches. Follow the same guidelines as those for larger bush roses. Remove dead, diseased, or weak wood; take out any crisscrossing canes; and open up the center of the plant. Up to six new and strong canes may be left on the plant after pruning.

Tree roses are pruned much the same way as bush roses, but keep in mind they are unattractive if they are not symmetrical. Prune canes to 12 inches in length, and leave them as evenly spaced around the plant as possible.

Polyantha roses are fairly hardy and seldom suffer any winter dieback. Prune them to about half their former height. They are vigorous plants, sending up many new canes each year. Prune the oldest ones each spring, leaving as many as eight on a plant. Like shrub roses, they are primarily grown for landscaping effect, so should be left on the full side.

Go easy in the first few years of a rose bush's life, pruning it on the light side until it is well established. In the first spring after it is planted, it will rarely be necessary to do more than remove weak, dead, or diseased wood; shape; and cut to size. In following years, old canes may be removed as new ones grow.

Pruning can be a scratchy chore, especially if large bushes and long canes are involved. For protection against marked arms and thorned fingers, wear long sleeves and a pair of heavy gloves. Watch what you wear, too, for some fabrics (nylon for one) catch on to the thorns much easier than others do.

Several weeks after you have pruned, take a walk through the garden with your shears. A late spring frost or other unexpected mishap may have caused some minor dieback on one or two canes. There might be a dead branch or two you missed the first time through. Just snip it off down to a good bud.

Although you will need the shears throughout the summer (to cut flowers from the plants), clean and oil them after pruning.

HOW TO PRUNE A CLIMBER

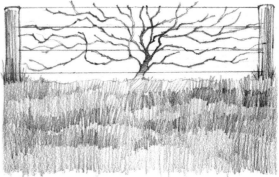

Climbers are pruned somewhat differently than bush roses. The majority of climbers bloom on old wood; the canes which grew the year before. Spring pruning chores should be limited to cutting out any wood that might have died over the winter or some last-minute shaping. Pruning done in early spring only results in cutting away all the flower buds.

After the climber has bloomed, remove one or two of the oldest canes to make room for new ones to grow. Thin out dense growth and shorten canes if the plant is too large. A rose grows where it is cut, so prune it back further than you want its final size to be. To get maximum bloom from most climbers, train canes horizontally along a fence, and secure them with plant ties.

How to Care for Roses

If you take care of your roses, they will reward you all summer with beautiful blooms. Take water as an example. Roses will survive with only a little but will do so much better with the right amount. Blooms will be larger, have more substance, better color, and last longer.

There is more than one way to water your roses. Sub-irrigation pipes may be installed underground, but this is not a method recommended for the home garden. Soaker hoses may be laid on the ground and the water allowed to trickle from their tiny holes. Because it may require the skill of an acrobat to move them around, they should be left in place all summer. The garden hose may be laid on the ground and the water allowed to run from it, or the roses may be watered by hand with a watering can or wand.

One of the easiest ways to water is with an overhead sprinkler. So long as it runs in the morning (wet leaves at night may become diseased), it is an excellent way to give needed moisture to your roses. There are also a few nice side effects of overhead watering. Spray residue is washed off the foliage, as is dust, and the high moisture will discourage spider mites.

Roses should be watered regularly, throughout the growing season, if the skies do not cooperate by providing rain. The equivalent of one inch of rain should fall on the rose garden each week. This will mean enough moisture for the entire root area to become wet. Sandy soils, which drain quickly, will need to be watered more often, and clay soils, which hold great amounts of water, will need watering less frequently. Soils that have had organic matter mixed in with them, as they should, will also retain moisture better than unimproved ones and do not need to be watered as often. Mulched gardens will also need less water than unmulched gardens.

Frequency of watering also depends on the weather. When the thermometer skyrockets, extra water will have to be applied. These rules apply to all plants and not just to roses, so don't think you have to be a slave to the garden hose. Water the roses when you water other flowers or the lawn, and they will respond.

If you are not sure when your roses need water, stick your finger into the soil as far as you can; if your fingernail hits dry soil, it's time to water. A rain gauge can also be installed as a guide. Whatever you do, water deeply; light sprinklings do more harm than good.

HOW TO CARE FOR ROSES

Spring is a time spent preparing for the roses of summer. As soon as weather permits, remove winter protection, prune, clean up, and apply a dormant spray of lime sulfur for insect and disease control.

Water is the most essential element you can give to your roses. If you have the time, water by hand with a wand, as illustrated. This is also an excellent way to relax and enjoy the rose garden on a summer evening.

Next to water, fertilizer is the best thing you can give to your roses. A balanced fertilizer, such as 5-10-5, or a prepared rose food, is the best bet. The first digit represents the percentage of nitrogen needed for growth and good, green leaves. The second is the amount of phosphorus, which ensures sturdy root growth and better flowers. The last number stands for the amount of potash, which is essential for plant vigor and food production.

Roses should be fertilized at least three times a year—right after pruning in early spring, just before the plants show their first bloom, and again two months before the first frost is expected. An alternative to this schedule is to fertilize once a month during the growing season, observing the same cutoff date for last feeding.

Apply the fertilizer, following label directions for the amount to use and spreading it over the entire root area, but not on the bud union. Lightly work into the top of the soil or the mulch, and water in well. Use twice the recommended amount for large shrub roses or climbers and a quarter to a half the amount for miniatures. Newly planted bushes should not be fed until they bloom.

Relatively new, slow release fertilizers give food to the plant when the soil is warm and stop feeding when temperatures drop. They may be used at the second feeding, eliminating the need to do further fertilizing that year. The mulch must be pushed aside, the fertilizer lightly scratched into the soil, and the mulch restored.

Liquid feeding is a marvelous way to give an instant boost to your plants, especially when they are coming into their first bloom. Mix one of the soluble fertilizers with water, and apply the solution with a watering can. If you have a lot of roses, a proportioning sprayer will be a great time-saver. You can apply the liquid to the roots or spray it on the leaves. Foliar feeding is recommended at any time the temperature is not over 90° Fahrenheit. Soluble food can also be mixed in with your fungicide or insecticide spray, thereby letting the spray do double duty.

Several other elements are needed for good growth. One is calcium, which you get with lime if you are raising the pH or from gypsum if the acidity does not need adjusting. Another is magnesium, present in dolomitic limestone. If leaves turn yellow, it might be a lack of iron.

It's possible to grow roses without mulching them, but they will be much better if you do. A mulch is simply a layer of material spread on top the soil. It keeps the soil cool and even tempered, conserves moisture, and keeps away the back-breaking chore of weeding. As it decomposes, it enriches the soil. Left in place all winter, it prevents the heaving of plants from the soil due to alternate freezing and thawing. Mulched roses will also be cleaner because the mulch prevents any soil from splattering the foliage during rainstorms.

Any number of organic mulches may be used; the only requirements are that they be light, permeable, and attractive. Try wood chips, pine needles, buckwheat hulls, cocoa bean shells, sawdust, or chopped oak leaves. Peat moss is not a good choice, because it gets crusty and is hard to wet; straw and hay are weedy; grass clippings, unless thinly dried, are slimy and mat down. If the material is fresh, apply extra nitrogen. Otherwise, the roses will be robbed of it as the mulch decomposes.

Once mulch is in place, it does not have to be removed in winter. If necessary, you can add to it the following year.

Besides mulch, another way to control invading weeds is with metal edgings. The metal will help keep grass and other weeds out of beds, making garden maintenance easier.

Spread fertilizer evenly around the root area, and work it lightly into the soil. If you have doubts about the condition of your loam, have a soil test done to see if it is lacking in any of the essential elements.

In mid-spring, after the ground is warm but before the weather becomes hot, apply a layer of mulch two to three inches thick. Do not let the mulch come in contact with the canes. Mulch will keep the soil cooler in summer.

How to Care for Roses

Keep an eye out for suckers, canes that grow from the understock beneath the bud union. They are easy to recognize because their foliage is quite distinct from that of the top part of the plant. If they ever reach the blooming stage, you'll see tiny white flowers (Rosa multiflower) or blooms of red (Dr. Huey). On tree roses, suckers can come from two locations—from the root stock or from the stem. Miniatures and some old garden and shrub roses are grown on their own roots, so suckers are not a problem and should not, of course, be removed.

DISBUDDING

If you want large flowers, one bloom to a stem, you will have to disbud. As soon as tiny buds are visible around the central bud or down the stem, remove them gently with your fingers or with the help of a narrow, pointed implement, a toothpick, for example. If you wait too long before disbudding, you will have a big black scar.

For a more attractive floribunda

spray, remove the central bud as soon as it forms. If you don't, the middle flower will be past its peak while the other flowers are in bloom or just opening; removing it then will leave a hole in the spray.

Some of the old garden roses—albas, centifolias, and moss roses in particular—can be pegged or pinned down at the end of the long canes. Not only will this make these large plants easier to control and more shrubby in appearance, it will also encourage the formation of more basal breaks.

DEADHEADING

Deadheading is the term applied to the removal of spent blooms from the rose bush. A good rule to follow is to cut the stem down to the first leaf with five leaflets, the point from which the next stem will grow and bloom. First-year plants, in particular, should be cut back only slightly at this time to encourage sturdy and vigorous growth.

When deadheading, taller and more vigorous plants may have a longer stem cut off, if you wish to shorten the bushes. Remember, though, that every time you cut off an extra leaf, you are cutting off a food-producing factory. Don't overdo it, or you will weaken the rose. Allow at least two leaves to stay on any cane—and preferably more.

Old blooms past their peak should be removed from the plant as soon as possible. Not only does this show off your good gardening and keep your beds free of fallen petals, it also encourages the plant to repeat its bloom more quickly.

Every rule has an exception and this one is no different. Shrubs, old garden roses, and climbers that bloom only once don't have to be deadheaded. Attractive hips of red or orange will form that will lure the birds and be used in recipes.

To keep climbers in bloom all summer, prune them as soon as their first flush of flowers is finished. Cut the lateral canes back, leaving two five-leaflet leaves on each. A new stem topped with a bloom will grow from each leaf axil.

Roses cut in bud or bloom, to be brought inside the house for flower arrangements, are handled in the same way as deadheaded flowers. Roses for arrangements should be disbudded. Cut the stems as long as you want, so long as two leaves are left on the main cane.

To keep those flowers large and beautiful and the plants vigorous and healthy, don't forget the soil. Roses grow best in a soil that is just slightly acid. Every few years, make sure the pH is at the right level.

PROTECTION

If you live in an area where winter temperatures drop below 20° Fahrenheit, take steps to protect your roses, especially the tender varieties.

Most climbers will withstand temperatures even lower than 20° without suffering severe damage. In sections where the cold reaches 0° Fahrenheit or lower, take climbers off

their supports, lay the canes on the ground, peg them down, and cover them up with oak leaves or soil, for example. In early spring, remove the protection and tie the climbers back up. An alternative to this is wrapping the canes in burlap while they are still attached to the supports, but this method can be cumbersome and much more difficult to manage.

Miniatures are tough plants and rarely need much protection, even in the coldest of climates. Raking leaves around and in between minis is the most they will ever need to get them through the winter. Shrubs and many of the old garden roses are very hardy and need no winter protection. This is a good thing, because most of them grow so large they would be impossible to protect. Polyanthas, too, are very hardy, withstanding the rigors of most any winter.

But the hybrid teas, grandifloras, and floribundas are not so independent and need your help to survive the cold if the thermometer reads below 20° Fahrenheit. This does not mean an occasional plunge in the temperature will harm your roses. Great fluctuations in temperature, extended periods of severe cold, and drying winds cause winter dieback. A deep layer of snow lying over the roses all winter is one of the best protections nature can provide.

Right after the ground has frozen is the perfect time to apply winter mulch. Use one of the methods illustrated below, or try something different. Rose cones made from plastic foam fit over the plants and keep out wind and cold. They should be saved for very cold areas or very tender plants, because the bush will have to be cut back severely for the cone to fit over it. Cones can also act like a greenhouse and cause premature growth during January thaws or other warm spells, growth that will undoubtedly die later.

Another good method of protection is evergreen boughs, and these are readily available in the form of unsold Christmas trees after the holidays are over.

Roses are not generally pruned in the fall. But if they grow particularly tall during the summer, cut them back before applying protection. This will prevent them from whipping in the wind or breaking under the weight of snow.

Protection during the winter is often not needed. If you are not sure which way to go because you live in a borderline area, protect those roses listed as tender. Most of the yellow roses, plus many pastel pinks and whites need protection.

Remove the protection when growth starts in the early spring, just before pruning. That prevents the new shoots from growing through the soil mound and becoming soft and brittle. But remember don't get itchy and remove winter mulch too early; a late frost may unexpectedly cause damage.

Remember that strong, healthy, well-cared-for bushes will fare better in winter than weak or neglected ones. Lush growth from the previous season that has not been hardened off is also susceptible to attack by the cold. This is why you shouldn't apply fertilizer after midsummer. By halting your rose bush feeding plan in mid-summer, you will allow plenty of time for the rose bushes to harden off and ready themselves for winter.

Move container roses to a frost-free spot. Wrap tree roses in burlap, lift, and move them indoors for the winter.

HOW TO OVERWINTER ROSES

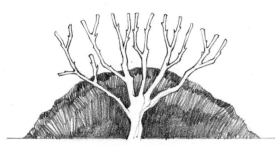

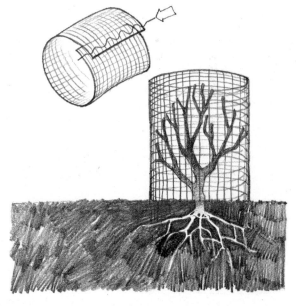

The traditional way to protect roses is to mound up soil over the canes, to a height of about 20 inches. The most important thing to do if you use this method is to bring soil in from another part of the garden. Don't take soil from around the plants, because this will expose delicate feeder roots to the cold air. In the spring, the soil will have to be removed from the plants and the beds and stored somewhere during the summer. Be sure to remove the soil from around the plants before the next season's growth begins. Young shoots are extremely tender and are easily damaged by rough treatment. To keep damage to a minimum, it's a good idea to first wash the soil mound away from the immediate vicinity of the crown of the plant with a gentle stream of water from the garden hose. Then, carefully scrape away the rest of the mound with a trowel or small spade. When the soil mound is removed, the bud union of the rose should be visible just above the ground level.

Once the soil has been removed, it's time to add several inches of mulch to increase soil moisture.

Another effective method of protecting your roses is to wrap a wire mesh cylinder around them and fill it with leaves. Make sure you choose a type of leaf that will not mat down and will allow water to drain through it. Oak leaves are perfect; maple leaves are to be avoided, at all costs. This rule also applies when you're raking leaves into rose beds to protect them during the winter. It's an easy method if you have the right trees.

Pests and Diseases

Unfortunately, pests and diseases enjoy our roses as much as we do. However, you don't have to let the garden become their home. The effectiveness of today's chemicals, the ease with which they're mixed, and the availability of modern equipment have made pest and disease prevention and control easy tasks.

Don't let the illustration on the opposite page alarm you. It shows all the pests and diseases that could possibly attack a rose. The chances of every one appearing at the same time in one garden are very small.

The question of spraying vs. dusting often arises. If you have only a few bushes, dusting is more convenient because no mixing is needed. Place the powder in the duster, and use when needed, without cleaning in between. On the other hand, spraying is more effective because coverage is more uniform.

What type of sprayer should you use? If you have a small number of plants, use a small bottle of the type used to mist indoor plants. Proportioning sprayers attach to the end of the garden hose and automatically dilute a concentrate as they spray, although the spray is coarse and not always uniform. There are sprayers that pump up; they're good but heavy. Electric or battery powered sprayers deliver a very fine mist but are impractical, except in large gardens. Whatever you use, clean it after every spray.

Spray to control insects. To prevent diseases, on the other hand, you must spray every ten days. Choose the right material for the job, handle it with care, and read the label. Rather than spraying twice, combine pesticides and fungicides in the same spray, or buy one of the combination sprays.

Systemics are great labor-saving materials that are absorbed by the plant to do their work from within. Apply them less often.

Starting at the lower left (opposite) and proceeding clockwise around the rose are potential pests and diseases and the recommended prevention or control:

Spider Mite This tiny creature is not an insect. It sucks life from the undersides of leaves. Foliage turns a dull red, and webs appear in advanced stages. If they become a problem, spray every three days with a rose miticide to kill new mites as they hatch. Mites also hate water, so mist the plants frequently.

Rose Scale This insect hides under a crusty white or gray shell and sucks sap from plants so they eventually wilt and die. Cut out infested areas, and apply a dormant lime sulfur spray in early spring. Use a commercial rose insecticide.

Fuller Rose Beetle This gray-brown insect munches on rose leaves, doing most of its damage while in the larval stage. Use a commercial rose insecticide.

Rose Slug This soft, yellow-green insect is actually the larva of one of the flies. It eats holes in the leaves and in time skeletonizes them. Use a commercial insecticide.

Rose Chafer A spiny-legged beetle with a grayish-brown cast, it feasts on flowers and leaves in early summer. Use a commercial insecticide.

Tarnished Plant Bug Not a frequent visitor to roses, this green to brown insect lays eggs along the stems and sucks juices from them. They can also carry disease.

Aphids Also called plant lice, they are green or brown sucking insects that colonize along buds and young shoots in spring. Luckily, they are easy to control with soapy water or a commercial insecticide.

Leaf Rollers These caterpillars roll themselves up in the foliage and eat through it from the inside out in spring. They also bore small holes into the base of the buds. Use a commercial insecticide.

Thrips These microscopic insects squirm between the petals of the bud and suck juices from it. Buds fail to open or produce distorted, brown flowers. Thrips favor white and pastel roses. Remove infested buds; use a commercial insecticide.

Midge A minute maggot causes sudden blackening of buds and young shoots, which should be cut off. Use a commercial insecticide.

Japanese Beetle Shiny copper and green insects eat holes in the flowers in midsummer, especially the varieties with lighter colors. Hand pick or spray with commercial insecticide. Grubs can be stopped with a rose insecticide applied to the soil.

Spotted Cucumber Beetle A yellow insect with 12 dark spots on its wing covers, it feeds on rose blooms from time to time. It also is a carrier of bacterial disease. Use a commercial insecticide.

Leaf Cutting Bee This bee bites neat, perfect circles in the margins of the leaves but luckily does not bother the blooms. Use a commercial insecticide.

Mildew This fungus disease is characterized by a white powder coating the leaves, which curl and become distorted in severe cases. Mildew occurs when days are warm, nights cool, and air circulation poor. Use a commercial fungicide.

Harlequin Bug A brightly colored red and black insect, mostly found in the South, sucks the leaves, leaving calico markings and causing wilt. Use a commercial insecticide.

Black Spot As the name suggests, this fungus disease causes round, black spots on the leaves. The leaves turn yellow and eventually fall off. The disease is spread by splashing water, so run sprinklers only in morning. Use a commercial fungicide.

Canker This fungus disease usually enters through wounds and causes canes to turn brown, purple, or white. Prune to below the canker in early spring, and apply a spray of dormant oil.

Rust Primarily confined to the Pacific coast, it causes orange spots on the undersides of leaves to appear in wet and mild weather. Use a commercial rose spray.

Cane Borer Boring insects can tunnel into canes or under bark. Where this is a problem, seal canes after pruning. Use a commercial insecticide.

Not illustrated, but potentially lethal, are nematodes, which are tiny animals that cause swellings on roots and cause stunted growth. Use an all-purpose rose spray that specificallly mentions nematodes. Crown gall is another underground problem, a bacterial disease that causes rough, round growth on the roots or bud union. Sorry, but remove the plant.

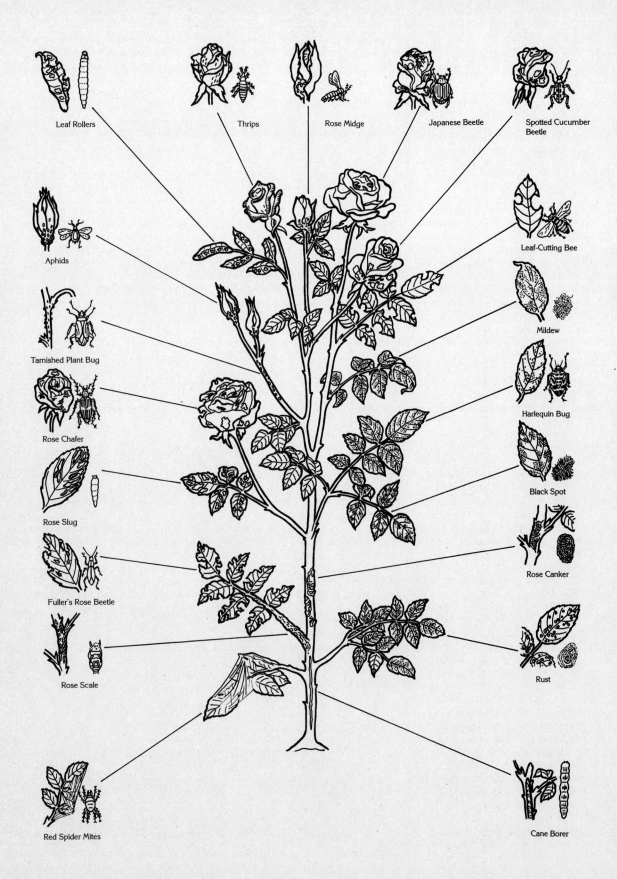

Leaf Rollers

Thrips

Rose Midge

Japanese Beetle

Spotted Cucumber
Beetle

Aphids

Leaf-Cutting Bee

Tarnished Plant Bug

Mildew

Rose Chafer

Harlequin Bug

Rose Slug

Black Spot

Fuller's Rose Beetle

Rose Canker

Rose Scale

Rust

Red Spider Mites

Cane Borer

How that Perfect Rose Happens

The top quality roses introduced every year are not just accidental finds made by rose growers. These new and improved varieties are products of years of observation, patient research, skill, and hard work by hybridizers in the United States and Europe. Luck plays a certain part in the development of an outstanding new rose, but few rose growers can depend on it. Research personnel must have intimate knowledge of which roses make good parents, which good (and bad) traits are passed on most frequently, and which combinations are most apt to produce the desired result.

These traits are the ones most gardeners want their roses to have: disease resistance, vigorous growth, long buds, a color breakthrough, abundant flowering, good foliage, hardiness, fragrance, perfect form. One quality doesn't make a good rose; the entire ensemble does. It sounds like a tall order for even one variety of rose. Yet hybridizers have accomplished the task time and again to give rose lovers satisfaction every year.

The road from creation to eventual introduction of a new variety is a long one, one demanding patience and perseverance. First, some of the crosses may not take. Those that do are sown and grown in the greenhouse where they are evaluated. The promising ones (about one percent) are chosen to be budded for further testing, and the rest are discarded.

The newly budded seedlings are then grown outdoors in field trials for at least two years and usually more. These new roses are viewed in the grower's own field, in public gardens, and often by homeowners in a diversity of climates.

Little by little, through the process of elimination, the field is narrowed to that special rose or roses that will be placed on the market. For every 30,000 seeds planted, chances are only one rose will ever be worth marketing. The odds are staggering to say the least.

Once a selection is made and a decision reached to introduce a new rose, it takes another two years to produce enough plants to sell. So, from the time the initial cross is made, through the greenhouse and outdoor testing, to the ultimate sale, at least seven, and more likely ten, years have passed.

Roses sold in this country are known as two-year plants, meaning that two years have gone by from the time the understock was planted to the harvesting of the new variety. Understock is planted one year, budded the next, and dug the following season. Although the understock is two years old, the new variety has been budded onto it for a little more than one year.

The exception to this process is the miniature rose. Although methods of crossing varieties to make new hybrids are essentially the same, minis are not budded but are grown on their own roots. For this reason, reproduction is quicker, and the testing and waiting period are not so long. Miniatures are propagated by stem cuttings taken after the flowers fade and the wood is hard. Minis will root in several weeks and bloom a few weeks later.

Like tends to beget like in the breeding of plants. When breeders set out to create a new rose, they have a definite goal in mind and select the parent plants with meticulous care. A great deal of time, money, and work will be involved, so they cannot afford a haphazard approach.

Breeding roses is an art, not a science, and involves an infinite number of possible offspring. For example, Charlotte Armstrong is a cross of Soeur Therese x Crimson Glory. You could cross these same roses forever and never come up with another Charlotte Armstrong. In fact, four seeds from the same hip could grow into four entirely different roses.

Charlotte Armstrong was widely used as a parent, however, and produced some famous offspring. Many other roses are used extensively as parents because they pass on desirable traits such as vigor, disease resistance, or fragrance. The offspring may appear with all the possible combinations of characteristics in the parents' backgrounds, but the hybridizer is after that one combination of traits that will give him the perfect rose. He may have to grow 30,000 seedlings to find it.

Below is a hypothetical example of breeding a perfect rose. There is no certainty this combination of parents will produce this rose, but it is possible. The uncertainty also breeds excitement.

Although it's highly unlikely that a home gardener could spare the time or the space needed to develop a new rose variety, it is possible to breed your own roses on a small scale. You might not develop a prizewinning rose, but you will learn a lot about your roses, their life cycle, and their genetic makeup. And most of all, by taking an active part in your rose growing, you will be better able to appreciate the magnificent accomplishment of the rose hybridizers and the modern rose. But before you start, be sure to read through the breeding guidelines shown on the following page.

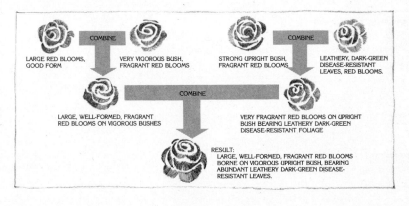

LARGE RED BLOOMS, GOOD FORM

COMBINE

VERY VIGOROUS BUSH, FRAGRANT RED BLOOMS

STRONG UPRIGHT BUSH, FRAGRANT RED BLOOMS

COMBINE

LEATHERY, DARK-GREEN DISEASE-RESISTANT LEAVES, RED BLOOMS.

COMBINE

LARGE, WELL-FORMED, FRAGRANT RED BLOOMS ON VIGOROUS BUSHES

VERY FRAGRANT RED BLOOMS ON UPRIGHT BUSH BEARING LEATHERY DARK-GREEN DISEASE-RESISTANT FOLIAGE

RESULT:
LARGE, WELL-FORMED, FRAGRANT RED BLOOMS BORNE ON VIGOROUS UPRIGHT BUSH, BEARING ABUNDANT LEATHERY DARK-GREEN DISEASE-RESISTANT LEAVES.

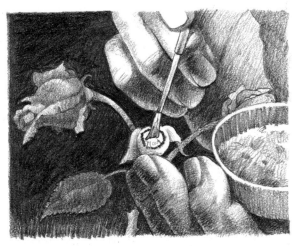

The first step in hybridizing consists of removing the yellow pollen-bearing stamens from the male parent. This is done with tweezers after removing the flower petals. Pollen is placed in a metal box or glass jar for drying and should be stored in the refrigerator. Stamens are removed from the female (seed-bearing) parent, and the rose head is bagged to avoid unintended pollination by insects or wind. When the stigma of the female parent is receptive, or sticky, pollen from the metal box is gathered on the tip of a camel's-hair brush or finger and is dusted on to induce the setting of seed. The bag is replaced for a week, and a record of the cross is made.

After the seed pod swells, matures, and turns red or orange, it is cut from the plant. Seeds are taken out of the hip and placed in a tightly closed can or plastic bag with a moistened germinating medium. They are then placed in the refrigerator to ripen for up to three months. Examine the seeds every two weeks, in case any start to sprout before the three months pass. If any do, remove them and plant them in a light soil mix. When the three months have passed, sow the seeds. When the new seedlings start to bloom (often within six weeks), the poor ones are culled, and the few good ones are saved and grown on—with high hopes.

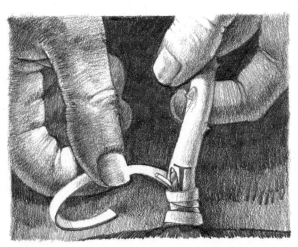

To multiply a promising seedling, a flowering stem is cut from the bush. This is known as budwood. Foliage is removed, leaving a short piece of leaf stem for a "handle." At the leaf axil (where the leaf joins the stem), there is a growth bud. The bud and the handle are both sliced from the stem and slid into a T-shaped slit that has been made in the bark of the understock plant near the soil level. This grafting process is referred to as budding. The bud is held firmly in place by a rubber band that keeps out air and prevents the bud from drying out. Budding is a delicate process, usually performed after the first flush of bloom is complete. If the bud fails to swell and turn green after being budded, a new bud can be added to the understock.

If the bud stays plump and green, the hybridizer knows it is alive and capable of growing (if it dries and shrivels after a week, he tries again). After the seedling bud is knitted in or making growth on its own, the whole top of the understock is cut back to within about ½ inch of the graft. From then on, the understock nurses the developing bud, which grows into a new bush that may eventually find its way into your garden. Test seedlings and commercially produced roses are budded onto understock, primarily of *R. multiflora* or Dr. Huey, to give them greater strength, vigor, and winter hardiness than they would have on their own roots. Then, only if the plants produce the expected results consistently in the field will it be grown commercially.

Arranging Roses

Arranging your roses will bring the beauty of the garden indoors and brighten up any room of the house. Whether it be a casual or a formal treatment, the bouquet is a living expression of your personality and love.

The easiest arrangement is not really an arrangement at all. One flower in a bud vase is simple yet elegant and can easily be changed to fit your mood.

Most arrangements you will show off in your home will combine several varieties of roses and several different types of garden flowers or both. Those same companions you combined with your roses in the planting beds look equally as beautiful sharing a vase. With roses, try iris, lilies, delphinium, gladiolus, veronica, snapdragons, astilbe, stock, asters, chrysanthemum, or daisies of any type. Don't be afraid to experiment with flower combinations that might seem a bit unorthodox.

Formal occasions demand subtle colors and close harmony; informal settings call for bolder and brighter contrasts, with more varied colors and flowers. Fit the roses, the design, and the container to the room or the mood of the occasion.

When choosing a container, keep two things in mind. First is size; the container must be in scale with the roses. Second is the material of the container. Roses generally are thought to be elegant flowers. So, they're perfect in silver, porcelain, crystal, or china vases or bowls. They will do equally well, though, in casual arrangements in pewter, metal, or ceramic containers, or straw baskets. Old teapots or sugar bowls are also possible choices.

You don't have to put your roses in a vase—a shallow container is also an attractive possibility. To anchor the flowers and keep them standing tall and straight, use a pinholder or florists' foam. If foam is your choice, soak completely in water before you place the roses in it. With either, keep the water supply steady and changed at least once a day. Nothing will shorten the life of an arrangement quicker than fouled water.

The popularity of miniature roses has led to a whole new sub-hobby—collecting miniature containers. To show them off in perfect scale, put your minis in thimbles, doll house furniture, seashells, shot glasses, or medicine bottles.

When choosing roses to arrange, pick fully double varieties for best results. Flowers with fewer petals open flat quickly and need to be replaced more frequently. In general, the more double the rose, the slower it will open and the longer it will last. Most shrub and old-fashioned roses wilt quickly and are therefore not good in arrangements, but don't overlook their foliage and hips as fillers and as backgrounds.

Foliage accompanying roses in arrangements is important, too, and needn't be rose leaves alone. For tall and spiking arrangements, try iris, gladiolus, or canna leaves. For variegated foliage, snip a few hosta leaves, or cut artemisia for a silver-gray effect. One of the broadleaved evergreens can be used for its shiny green foliage. For delicacy and grace, try ivy or asparagus ferns. At Christmastime, combine roses with holly berries and sprigs of pine or yew.

The art of arranging roses involves organizing flowers, container, and accessories according to principles of design. The result should be simple, beautiful, expressive, and harmonious in detail.

To achieve these results, your arrangement should appeal to the senses, be pleasing in space, line, form, pattern, texture and color. Even fragrance should be considered. A too strongly scented arrangement can easily become overpowering.

Space available will determine the size and shape of the arrangement. A design for a buffet table should be low and long; that for a pedestal should be upright. Fill the space as though you were filling a picture frame. With line, the eye moves from one part of the arrangement to the others. Line may be long or short, straight or curved, delicate or bold, horizontal or vertical, so long as it is there.

Think of form when arranging your roses. This means thinking in three dimensions and not just height and width. This is very critical if the design is viewed from all sides of the room.

Within the form, the roses need to be arranged in a creative pattern. This can be achieved by the repetition of certain varieties or colors in a mass arrangement or by careful placement of the flowers, leaving open spaces between them.

Texture of the container, foliage, other flowers, and accessory material must be in character with the form and color of the roses. A fine-textured porcelain vase demands a delicate, light arrangement, while a design in a cast-iron kettle takes stronger colors and a heavier touch.

Color is perhaps the most important element of design and is inseparable from it. Color causes a psychological reaction, a sensation of the soul.

Choose your colors carefully to express your emotions. Your arrangement can be of various shades and tints of the same color, of closely related colors, or of opposite colors. For example, if yellow is your color, the arrangement can be of lemon through gold, or yellow with yellow-orange and orange, or yellow with mauve.

Use the elements of design in the right way, and your arrangement will be balanced. This does not necessarily mean it will be symmetrical; it means it will be in equilibrium. To assist in achieving balance, place buds toward the top and fuller roses toward the bottom. Darker colors should also weight the bottom. If the container is stronger on one side, the arrangement should be balanced in the same direction.

The last feature your design should have is rhythm. The eye must be carried easily from one part of the arrangement to another. This can be achieved by repetition of color or form, by progressing from bud to full open flower, or by the line.

Flower arranging is an art, not a science, and can be a very fulfilling sideline for rose growers. After a little practice, you'll be making flower arrangements for the porch or patio, the bathroom, the guest room. Your design will brighten up dark corners, mantels, pianos, the table. Formal or natural, let it be creative!

Deep red roses in a crystal vase spell refinement, elegance, and dignity.

Arranging Roses

The only color on this table is that of the roses, making a dramatic contrast to the black and white of the china and accessories.

Just because it's winter doesn't mean you have to be without roses for the house or table. The same care you gave to roses from the garden should be given to those bought in a store. As soon as you get them home, re-cut them under water and store them in water in a cool place for several hours before making the arrangement.

Should your roses prematurely wilt, revive them by cutting the stems under water and placing the roses in a bucket of lukewarm water, up to the neck of the flower, for several hours.

If your arrangement is going to be viewed from all sides, be sure it is equally attractive all around. To make this task easy, put your arrangement together on something that revolves, a Lazy Susan, for instance.

And if your arrangement will be set close to the viewers, pick roses for their fragrance as well as their eye appeal. Also, don't overlook the effect that white or colored light will have on bringing out the tones and luster of the cut roses. Adjust it as needed, but be careful you don't overdo the effect.

Dried blue-violet statice enhance the beauty of pink roses.

Sing 'Auld Lang Syne' with a holiday arrangement of greens.

How to Handle Cut Flowers

One of the joys of growing roses is being able to go outside and cut a bouquet of fresh flowers. Many of your favorite roses are not available in the florist's shop. Besides, it's fun to choose flowers for the house to carry out a color scheme.

Like all trades, there are tricks and tools. Before snipping, read these basics to ensure a professional and long-lasting arrangement.

For best results, cut stems from well-watered plants late in the afternoon. Place roses into water immediately (so carry a pail of water with you into the garden). If this is impossible, carry the roses head-down, and place them in water as soon as you can. Do not use cold water directly from the garden hose.

Cut the stems at an angle, and put them into lukewarm water up to the neck of the flower. After you have finished cutting, re-cut all stems under water to fill them with moisture. Place the pail with the roses in a cool, dark spot until the water cools to room temperature—for several hours or, better yet, overnight—before arranging the cut flowers. Roses may also be "conditioned" in the refrigerator if they don't have to share it with culinary delights.

Before the roses are arranged, the foliage should be cleaned. Stubborn spray residue or mildew can be washed away with soap and water and rinsed clean. Leaves can be made to shine, naturally, by rubbing them with a paper towel or discarded pantyhose. Should a leaf be ripped or chewed by a crawling friend or enemy, it can easily be trimmed with a pair of manicure scissors.

One important factor in the good looks and long life of your bouquet is the choice of flowers. Avoid buds too tight or blooms past their peak.

The roses sketched above are good examples of a bud that's too tight (left); a rose at the perfect stage

for cutting (center), with the sepals down; and a fully open flower that will soon wilt or shatter and spoil the appearance of your arrangement. Some roses at this advanced stage may, however, be floated on water inside a rounded glass bowl or brandy snifter. They will remain attractive for several days if you freshen the water daily.

When you are selecting roses for the house, remember that future bloom depends on how you go about cutting. Although it's tempting to snip very long stems, leave at least two healthy five-leaflet leaves on the remaining stem to help the plant maintain its strength and vigor.

To save pricked fingers when arranging roses, hold stems high and clip off all thorns wherever you have to touch the stems.

For roses, or any cut flower for that matter, clip off all foliage that would be below the water level in the finished arrangement. Such leaves would quickly disintegrate, foul the water, and shorten the life of your arrangement.

To lengthen the life of your cut flowers, add a floral preservative to the water, and change the water daily if feasible. If roses are in foam and changing water is not possible, at the very least add water every day to ensure freshness.

Roses open quickly once they're cut and brought indoors. To slow the opening, use florist's tape to hold the blooms gently shut until just before

the arrangement is put on view. To help further, keep the arrangement in a cool place, out of sunlight, and away from drafts and air conditioners to prevent the flowers from dehydrating and falling off the stems. With this type of common sense care, you can enjoy cut roses indoors from early summer right up until frost.

Preserving

Enjoy the beauty and pleasure of your rose garden long after autumn leaves have fallen and plants have faded from bloom by preserving it, drying it, and even eating it.

For potpourris and rose recipes, use only fragrant petals and hips cut from plants that have not been sprayed with pesticides. Gather the petals in the morning after the dew is gone, and remove the green or white base from the petals; known as the heel, it has a bitter taste. Rinse the petals lightly and pat dry with a paper towel.

Potpourri

Take the cover off a potpourri jar, and fill the room with the pleasant fragrance of roses and spices.

There are two types of potpourri: dried and moist. The same recipe can be used for either; only the method varies. Moist potpourri has a heavier scent and lasts for many years.

For dried potpourri, pick roses in the morning after the dew has lifted, when they are one-third to one-half open. Place the petals on screens or trays in a dry, airy room away from the sun, turning every day until they are crisp.

Dry petals all summer, storing them in dark, airtight containers. When you've collected enough, mix one tablespoon of fixative (orris or storax, for example) and one tablespoon of spices like cinnamon, mace, cloves, or allspice, with every quart of rose petals. Add other dry ingredients to the mixture—dried and crushed citrus peel, rose leaves, lavender, lemon balm, heliotrope, and rosemary. Add a few drops of fragrant oil, mix well, and age for six weeks.

For moist potpourri, dry rose petals until they are limp. In a jar, alternate ½-inch layers of petals with one tablespoon of non-iodized salt. After two weeks, add spices, fragrant oil, and partially dried flowers. Age for a month or more until the fragrance satisfies you completely.

Dried Roses

Color your home with dried roses long after the garden has faded from bloom.

For drying, pick dry flowers (not wet with rain or dew) in the stage of bloom you want to preserve.

Place a base of one to two inches of silica gel granules in the bottom of a cookie tin or coffee can, and insert the short cut stem of the flower, face up in the drying medium. Be careful not to overlap any of the petals between flower specimens. Gently sprinkle more of the granules over the flowers until they are completely covered with silica gel to a depth of about one inch. Cover tightly, and tape the name of the flower and the date on top of the container. Leave the tin in a dark, dry place for the required drying time (from two to six days). If in doubt, lift the lid and check. The petals should feel brittle and papery; if they don't, replace cover and let the flowers dry longer. When they are ready to remove, slowly pour off the silica gel, and cup your hand under the flower head. Shake off the drying compound gently, and, if necessary, remove stubborn granules with a soft artist's brush. Store the flowers in airtight boxes until ready to use. For neat storage, insert the erect stem ends in blocks of dry floral foam. To keep dried material in top condition, especially over prolonged periods or when excessive humidity may be a problem, add three to four tablespoons of silica gel to the storage container. If a petal falls off, use a toothpick to dab a small amount of white glue on the end of the petal, and, with tweezers, join it to the flower center. Don't forget to dry flower buds and leaves to enhance your arrangements. Dark red flowers aren't suitable for drying because they turn black.

Silica gel, available at craft shops, can be reused indefinitely but must be heated in the oven at 250 degrees Fahrenheit for one hour to restore the blue crystals to full potency.

Pressed

The avid pressed-flower enthusiast can buy a flower press, complete with blotting paper, at a craft shop. For the average pressed-flower lover, however, a thick telephone book will suffice. At one-inch intervals in the book, spread facial tissue on newspaper. Place the flowers flat. Avoid overlapping. Cover the flowers with tissue, then newspaper. In this way, the newsprint will not be picked up by the flowers while they're being pressed. Repeat the process until the book is filled. If possible, use materials of even thickness on each page for even drying. Remember to include buds, and curve some stems and leaves for graceful positioning when dried. Put a weight on the book, and store for three to four weeks away from sunlight in a dark, dry place.

Attar of Roses

Fill an earthen jar with rose petals, cover with water, and set in the sun. After one week, the oil will form on the surface. Soak up with a cotton swab and squeeze into a vial. For best results, use Damask rose petals.

Rose Beads

Years ago, young brides had their wedding bouquets made into rosary beads to remind them of their special day and to freshen newly stored linens.

Mix 1¾ cups of flour with four tablespoons of salt and enough water to make a smooth dough. Press into this mixture three cups of finely chopped, fragrant rose petals. Flour a bread board, and roll out the dough ¼ inch thick. Cut out circles with a thimble, and roll them into beads. String with wire, and hang in the dark until the beads are dry. Then re-string them to get the finished product. Beads will dry to brown unless they're colored with three drops of oil paint. Add ten drops of rose oil to increase the fragrance.

Rose Frosting

Mix three ounces of cream cheese with one tablespoon of milk. Sift 2½ cups of confectioners' sugar, and add it gradually, blending well. Add one teaspoon of rose water and food coloring, if desired. Spread the frosting on the cake, and sprinkle with chopped nuts. For best flavor, serve the cake chilled.

To make a potpourri mix pleasing to the eye as well as the nose, add some dried whole flowers for color.

Roses and Climate

There's more to roses than height or color. When you select yours, think also of winter weather. Some roses are too tender to survive deep freezes.

If your climate is mild, you're lucky; you can grow almost any rose there is. Where temperatures do not go below freezing, you can grow anything, including tree roses, tea and china roses, and noisettes without protection. In areas where temperatures drop to 20° Fahrenheit, protect tender hybrid teas, floribundas, and grandifloras.

Miniatures are happy, as are most climbers, without protection if the thermometer does not go below zero. Polyanthas, too, will survive this mark, but other modern roses must be protected to be safe.

If your climate is colder than this, you may want to rely on the old garden or shrub roses. They will withstand cold to −10° Fahrenheit, and the centifolias, damask, and kordesii will take temperatures even lower than that, to −20°.

These temperatures are to be used as general guidelines, as are the lines on the map. Temperatures may vary by as much as 5° Fahrenheit. Local conditions must also be considered. Being on a hill, in a valley, or in the protection of a windbreak may affect what you can grow. In general, you can also gamble and win in growing roses outside of your hardiness zone if snow or rainfall is high.

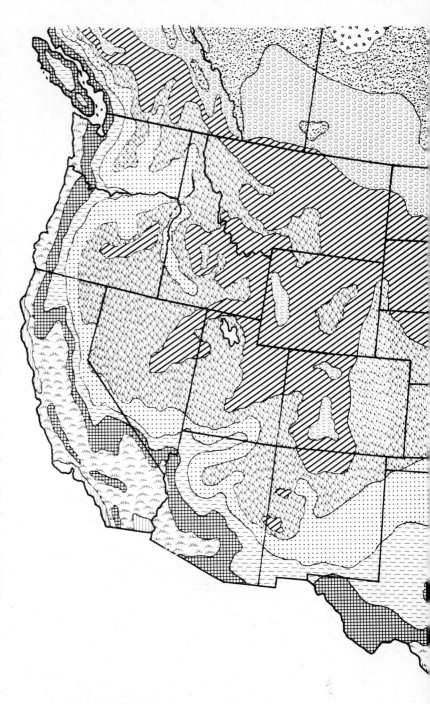

Source: United States Department of Agriculture

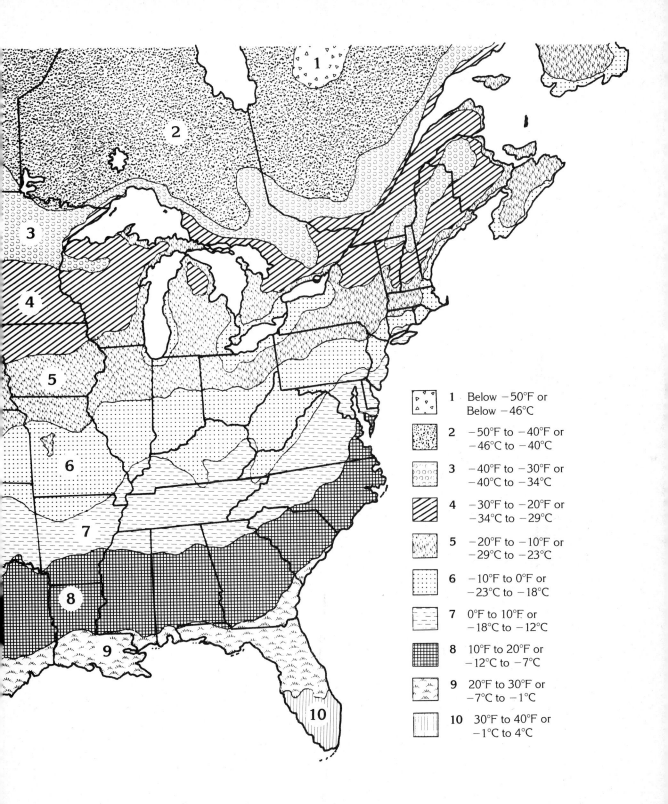

1   Below −50°F or
       Below −46°C

2   −50°F to −40°F or
       −46°C to −40°C

3   −40°F to −30°F or
       −40°C to −34°C

4   −30°F to −20°F or
       −34°C to −29°C

5   −20°F to −10°F or
       −29°C to −23°C

6   −10°F to 0°F or
       −23°C to −18°C

7   0°F to 10°F or
       −18°C to −12°C

8   10°F to 20°F or
       −12°C to −7°C

9   20°F to 30°F or
       −7°C to −1°C

10   30°F to 40°F or
       −1°C to 4°C

INDEX